Skellig

island outpost of Europe

DES LAVELLE

Skellig
island outpost of Europe

DES LAVELLE

THE O'BRIEN PRESS

11 Clare Street, Dublin 2, Ireland

Skellig

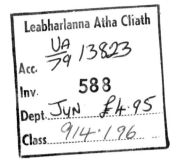
First published 1976
Second edition 1977
The O'Brien Press
11 Clare Street Dublin 2 Ireland
ISBN 0 905140 26 5

Cover design Jarlath Hayes

Maps Susan Hayes

Layout Michael O'Brien

Typesetting The Red Setter Ltd.

Printed by E. & T. O'Brien Ltd.
11 Clare Street Dublin 2. Ireland

Contents

Foreword

The two Skellig islands are many times more important than either their size or location would suggest. In any world map of Archaeology, the SKELLIG stands out in bold, conspicuous letters; similarly, in the Ornithological world, the name of SKELLIG conveys a richness of seabird life which is not easily equalled. These are but two aspects of an exciting pair of islands, yet, in sharp contrast with the neighbouring Blasket island, the Skellig has reached this day and age without a book to its name!

A vacuum of this intensity calls out for release — calls out for an effort to gather all the valuable fact, and equally valuable fiction of Skellig under one cover. But that is only part of the motivation for this book; the real reason is that these Skellig islands fascinate me. I have sailed around them, flown over them and dived on every sheer under-water cliff face beneath them; I have visited them to wander and wonder at least forty times in 1975, and the same the year before, and the year before... and by researching and writing and poring over a wide variety of photographs, I can be out there immediately in spirit, savouring, as George Bernard Shaw said about the place — "the magic that takes you out, far out, of this time and this world".

These spiritual visits are too wonderful to hide; I want to share them. But one must try to strike a balance of interest for the historian, the bird lover, the archaeological student, the day-visitor who needs an answer to a multitude of questions and the Kerryman who hungers for more knowledge of his native ground.

On the other hand, if I have omitted or misinterpreted any vital points — particularly in the realm of local history and custom — and if this publication evokes the hidden gems, I shall be happy with my work.

Elsewhere in the book I have named the many individuals and Services to whom I am indebted for their time, their interest and their assistance throughout the entire project, but I was fortunate to have one particularly steadfast and encouraging helper on my side from the outset — my all-enduring wife. For this reason, I dedicate the book: to Pat.

Des Lavelle, Valentia Island

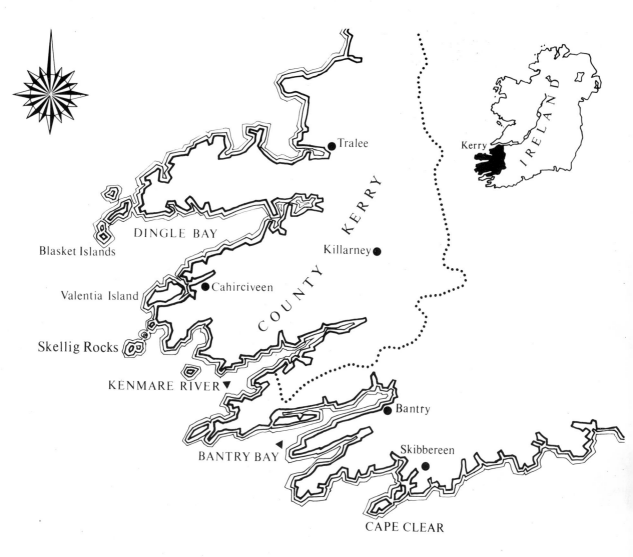

Tralee

Kerry

I R E L A N D

K E R R Y

Killarney

DINGLE BAY

Blasket Islands

Valentia Island

Cahirciveen

C O U N T Y

Skellig Rocks

KENMARE RIVER ▼

Bantry

BANTRY BAY ▲

Skibbereen

CAPE CLEAR

Skellig Michael
LOCATION MAP

0   10   20   30
scale in miles

Acknowledgements

The author has been helped along over the years by many people, and would like to thank in particular the following:

Miss M. O'Brien, Librarian, Cahirciveen; Miss K. Turner, Kerry County Library; Mr. T. Armitage, Central Library; Mr. F. J. Ryan, Skerries; Mr. T. Shortt, Cahirciveen; Mr. J. Shanahan, Portmagee; Mr. T. 'Busty' Burns, Valentia; Mr. P. O'Sullivan, C.B.S., Cahirciveen; Mr. J. O'Reilly, Cork; Mr. A. Lidstrom, Umea, Sweden; Mr. P. Gallagher, Hon. Secretary, Valentia Lifeboat; Mr. Don Roberts, Kilkenny; The Secretary, Irish Wildbird Conservancy; Mr. P. Evans and Mr. A. Lack of the B.T.O., for bird-counts and plant-lists; The Secretary and the Engineer in Chief, Commissioners of Irish Lights; The Principal and Assistant Keepers, Skellig Lighthouse; The Board of Trinity College Dublin; The Officers of the Royal Irish Academy; The Librarian, Bodelian Library, Oxford; The Archivist, Dept. of Irish Folklore, U.C.D., and the Directors of the National Museums of Dublin, Copenhagen and Oslo.

Photographic and darkroom facilities and much valuable advice on that subject were given by Padraig Kennelly, Tralee and Robin Holder, Valentia Island.

ABOUT THE PHOTOGRAPHS

All the photographs — except where otherwise accredited — are by the author, shot over the years 1972/75, with a Pentax Spotmatic and three lenses: 50mm., 28mm., and 135mm. The films used included Kodak Tri X and Plus X but the great majority of the prints used here were "wrung out" in Black and White from Kodacolor X negatives.

Early History and Legend

"ike two mighty ships, sailing along majestically with every shred of canvas set"; such are the Skellig Rocks — Skellig Michael and Small Skellig — eight and a half miles off Valentia on the Atlantic coast of Kerry. These great towering sea-crags, steeped as they are in history and legend, become daily more and more important in this particular age of bustle, pollution and all-consuming "progress". The archaeology of Skellig, the bird life, the seals, the wide-open, timeless scenery; for one reason or another there is a balm for every soul on the Skelligs.

A shipwreck of some 1,400 B.C., brought about by the magic of the Tuatha de Danann, is our first reference to Skellig, when Melisius, leader of the early invasions of Ireland, lost two sons in the area.

"Irr lost his life upon the western main;

Skellig's high cliffs the heroe's bones contain.

In the same wreck Arranan too was lost,

Nor did his corpse e'er touch Ierne's coast."

Another legendary visitor of some importance about the year 200 A.D. was Daire Domhain — King of the World. He rested a while at the Skellig before his attack on the nearby coast, and his battle of a year-and-a-day with Fionn Mac Cool's Fianna at Ventry.

In the 5th century, Duagh, King of Munster, fled for his life to the isolation of the Skellig when pursued by Aengus, King of Cashel and another legend tells that St. Malachy, when driven from his monastery in Bangor, also fled to Skellig for refuge.

And what a real place of refuge this is! Landing on the smaller

Skellig is generally impossible, and on the larger, twin-pinnacled Skellig Michael — even granted that a landing may be possible — it still calls for a stout heart and a steady head to master the island's steep faces of shaly sandstone which reach 714 ft. in height.

Little wonder that this island like other similar high places became dedicated to Michael, Archangel, taking on the name by which it is known today, 'Sceilig Mhichíl'.

It was here, says the legend, on this "certain crag surrounded on every side by the eddies of the great sea... distant a day's sail from the land", that St. Michael appeared together with others of the Heavenly Host to help St. Patrick banish the serpents and other evil things of Ireland into the sea. And with relatively early Christianity came the founding of a monastery on the rock — a small enclosure of stone huts and oratories which, though long since unoccupied, still stand to this day near the island's Northern pinnacle, some 600 ft. above the sea.

The founder of this monastery is not named. Current tradition — without any supporting evidence — attributes it to one of two St. Finians, and the influence of "Finan" is certainly strong in local place-names, but another, seldom-mentioned, possible founder member of the monastic community is St. Suibhne of Skellig who is listed under April 28th in the Martyrology of Tallaght which was written at the end of the 8th century. Neither is the exact date of the foundation known, but the style of building suggests the 6th century onwards. There are other examples of this style and this date at many points of Ireland's West coast — but none in the area in such perfect repair as the Skellig Michael monastery.

In 795 A.D. the first Viking attacks from Scandinavia were launched on the Irish coast, and the Skellig settlement did not escape for long. The early Irish manuscripts, the *Annals of Innisfallen, Annals of Ulster* and *Annals of the Four Masters,* contain only scant information on these raids, and there are no written sources in Scandinavia from the Viking period, but we do know these sleek, clinker-built long-ships, with their high graceful bow and shallow draught were of advanced design in their age; some of them had a crew of 40, but others were big vessels of up to 135 ft. which could be rowed or sailed at 10 knots and could carry several hundred men.

In 812 A.D., the Skellig monastery was sacked. Again in 823, as reported in the *Annals of Ulster* and *Annals of Innisfallen,* the Vikings came and this time they took Eitgal, Abbot of Skellig, and starved him to death. The years 833 and 839 A.D., saw further attacks when Turgesius, Sovereign of the Danes, swept through the area.

Newman, in his Historical Sketches, gives a grim description of the Viking's technique:
"the sea, instead of being a barrier, was the very element and condi-

Left — Annals of Innis-
fallen. Bodelian Library.
ms. Rawl. B.503. f.14 r.
mid column 3, in Irish:
"Skellig was plundered by
the heathen and Etgal was
carried off and he died of
hunger on their hands.

Below— Annals of Ulster. T.C.D. ms. 1282. f. 38v. Col. 2. Lines three and four, in Latin: Eitgal of
Skellig was carried off by foreigners and he died of hunger and thirst.

tion of his victories and it carried him upon its bosom, up and down, with an ease and expedition which even in open country was impracticable. They ravaged far and wide at will, and no retaliation on them was possible, for these pirates, unlike their more civilised brethren of Algiers or Greece, had not a yard of territory, a town, or a fort, no property but their vessels, no subjects but their crews. They were not allowed either to inherit or transmit the booty which these piratical expeditions collected.... 'Never to sleep under a smoke-burnished roof, never to fill the cup over a cheerful hearth' was their boast and principle. If they drank, it was not for good company but by degrading extravagance, to rival the beasts of prey and blood in their wild brutality''.

Foley adds: "They ran into land and set fire to villages and massacred the inhabitants. Whilst so engaged, their favourite sport was the tossing of infants on top of their lances to and from each other.... Laws, religion and society they had no regard for. Both on sea and land their hands were always steeped in blood, murder and plunder. It was only when these pirates plundered and murdered each other that they finally collapsed''.

But in spite of the attacks and the plundering, the monastic community on Skellig survived, and in 860 A.D. some rebuilding was done. In the year 885 Flan MacCallach, Abbot of Skellig, died. In 950 A.D. the *Annals of the Four Masters* has the brief entry that Blathmac of Skellig passed away. In 993, legend tells that Viking Olav Trygvasson, who was later to become King of Norway and whose son, Olav II, was to become Patron Saint, was baptised by a Skellig hermit. The final report in this era, from the *Annals of the Four Masters,* dated 1044, tells simply: "Aodh of Skellig died''. This is all the information we have from that period.

How these ascetic monks ever contrived to live on this island is a mystery by today's standards. In summer, no doubt, they enjoyed seabirds, eggs and fish but winter must have brought months of lean isolation. The small hide-covered boats of the period were hardly adequate for a regular supply ferry; perhaps there was more arable soil on this 44 acre crag in olden times than there is today.

Sadly, few artifacts have ever come to light to give us any insight into the occupations of the Skellig monastic community. During the early lighthouse work in the 19th century two items were reported — but they were not retained, nor was their age discussed:
"Here we saw a small bronze figure of our Saviour, about four inches in height, found by the workmen in excavating. It was impossible to conceive anything more barbarous than this image, or nearer in resemblance to the rudest idol''. Another version says: "A rude bronze crucifix, with crown and kilted tunic, about four inches high, was found among the huts by the lighthouse workmen...'' and "We were

Above— Annals of the Four Masters. R.I.A. C3. 422v., in Irish
Line 1   A.D. 1044.
Line 5   Aodh of Skellig Michael died

Below— Annals of the Four Masters. R.I.A. C3 419v., in Irish:
Line 1:   A.D. 950.
End of line 4: Blathmac of Skellig died.

15

Above— A stone water-font from Skellig. It was in the large oratory during all living memory, but is currently retained in the lighthouse for safety. Its date is thought to be 17th century, and its measurements are: Front 7¾"; Side 5"; Height 4½".

Opposite Page— There are no written reports in Scandinavia from the Viking period, but excavated renovated artifacts, like this "Oseberg" Viking ship, speak eloquently for the ship-building skills of that era.

told of a clay figure of the Virgin, which had also been recently discovered".

A stone 'water-font', some 7¾" x 5" x 4½", which has been in the large oratory of Skellig monastery during all living memory is currently retained in the lighthouse for safe-keeping. It is thought to be late 17th or 18th century by the National Museum of Ireland, and its presence on Skellig is not clearly understood.

It is pleasant to dream that Skellig manuscripts similar to the Book of Kells or the other Irish Annals might exist and one day be discovered — but the harsh realities of the island must favour other conclusions: with minimal domestic equipment and few, if any, personal possessions other than the smock and cloak which they wore, membership of the Skellig monastery must have been a hard exercise in mere survival alone.

Giraldus Cambrensis — Welsh cleric and historian — reported at the end of the 12th century that the Skellig community moved base to Ballinskelligs "on the continent", but the island monastery did remain occupied and in repair, and it is a fact that one particular church building in the monastic enclosure was added in those middle ages. The ecclesiastical taxation of 1300 A.D. refers to the "Church of St. Michael's Rock" having a valuation of 20 sh.

Pilgrimage

ccupied or otherwise, Skellig Michael featured as a place of pilgrimage and penance for many years. Early in the 16th century the Register of Primate Dowdall of Armagh lists Skellig Michael as one of the principal penitential stations for the performance of public penance, and there is a record too of one sinner who was obliged to make a visit to the Skellig and other penitential stations as penance for murdering his own son.

Two centuries later writers such as Friar O'Sullivan were still referring to Skellig Michael, and to pilgrims coming from all over Ireland and Europe at Eastertime — not so much to visit the monastery, it would appear, but to perform the nerve-racking, difficult climb to follow the Stations of the Cross and finally kiss a stone carving over-hanging the sea at the "Needle's Eye", the 714 ft. western pinnacle of the island.

Early writers report the climax of this climb in great detail, describing the pilgrim inching his way outwards astride a narrow pro-jecting spit of rock, reciting certain prayers and finally kissing the carving at the extremity before retiring to safety. However, all these descriptions are greatly exaggerated, or the spur in question has fallen away, because at the summit today, there is only one overhanging spur — with a standing slab at its extremity — which, although certain-ly fearsome, projects not over the sea but Eastwards towards the Christ's Saddle area.

§ The Cowe and the Calfe.

§ THE WEST OCCEAN

Biar head.

O Iole

The sounde of Blaskay

uan

Biar castell

bier

Biar haven.

Croke.

O

Croke haven.

Sole

uan

more.

The sounde of Dorsey

The bay of dingle

The knight of Kiery

Lymericke haven

Mc Morish

O conor

Tral

Belatymore Cape clere

haven

THE

SPANISH

O driscol

The Erle of

Toohe clene

Clancary.

Iland

Erle of To monde

Mc Con

Mc Carty reugh

Rosse haven

Rosse

MO

NST

ER

Erle of Desmond

Knight of valley

Mc Brien

Molinge bay

The olde head

L: Courly

Kinsale haven

L: Bary oge.

Vicont Barymore

Lord Roche

SEA

Corke haven

cork beg

Clone

white

knight

SOVTH

Youghel haven

Dongurvan haven

Tramon bay

Water forde

Erle of Ormod

Kilkeny

LEINSTER

The haven

Rosse

Sylley

The cartographer of 1567 confuses the Blasket Sound and the Dursey Sound, but nonetheless the two Skellig Islands can be clearly recognised (marked with arrow at top of map).

"There is still living a gentleman", wrote Chatterton in 1839, "who *walked* out to the eternity of this spit, and performing a regular pirouette, *returned*! However, the guides always encouraged the pilgrims by assuring them that no one was ever lost but an Englishman, who undertook the pilgrimage in order to ridicule the custom, and falling from the spit was drowned. From this circumstance a saying, much in use in this country, as applied to persons of ridiculously inordinate desires, has its origins. It runs thus: 'More water', arsa an Sasanach agus é á bhádhaidh', or *'More water, says the Englishman and he drowning'*. The tradition being that the unfortunate Sasanach found himself so long falling, as to call out for the rising of the sea in order to put an end to his tumble".

Charles Smith, in his *Ancient and Present State of the County of Kerry,* 1756, shows a reproduction of "The Skellig from the South West", but its gross inaccuracy proves clearly that the artist was never near the rock. Descriptions of the monastery wells being "a few yards above sea level", when in fact they are at a height of some 600 ft. lead to a similar conclusion. On the other hand, the general difficulty of the climb to the "Needle's Eye" is very real, and due to looseness caused by the burrowings of a plague of rabbits, it is probably more hazardous now than ever before.

In August, 1779, one famous seaman, who certainly was no repentant pilgrim, almost came to grief upon the Skellig. The French Archives contain details from the Admiral's own pen: "At 8.00 p.m. Mizen Head lay astern, and with a fine breeze the squadron stood N.N.W. along the ironbound coast of Kerry. By noon we were five miles S.S.W. of Great Skellig".

Here the fleet ran into a calm, and after some time the Admiral's flagship began to drift dangerously close to the Skellig — so close that her largest rowing boat had to be lowered to tow her clear. But the tale does not end there. The oarsmen were all Irishmen who had been "pressed into service" against their wishes, and as soon as the flagship was out of danger — but still becalmed — they cut the tow rope and headed for Valentia at their best speed.

The flagship they had abandoned at the Skellig was the 42-gun *Bonhomme Richard* and the Admiral they had outwitted was that Master Privateer, John Paul Jones.

Early in the 19th century, on the annual Feast of St. Michael, the Parish Priest of Ballinskelligs, Fr. Diarmuid O'Sullivan, used to visit Skellig Michael by boat to offer Mass on the island. Many people would travel with the priest on this pilgrimage, and the details of one particular visit which was marred by a sudden gale have been handed down in verse by the Iveragh poet, Tomás Ruadh Ua Suilliobháin — 1785-1848.

Above — Skellig Michael from the South. The monastery is situated near the right-hand peak and the modern lighthouse is near the left foreground.

Below — The erroneous impression of Skellig Michael from Smith's *The Ancient and Present State of the County of Kerry.*

A View of the Great SCELIG ISLAND from the South West.

maiⓂean boᵹ, áluinn, i mbáiⓂ na sceaⓁᵹ

I

MaiⓂean boᵹ, áluinn, i mbáiⓂ na SceaⓁᵹ,
  Ⓓul aᵹ triall ċum Aiffinn ᵹráⓂṁaiⓇ Ⓓé,
Ⓓ'éiⓇiᵹ an truail Ⓡó-ṁóⓇ 'Ⓡan bḟaiⓇⓇᵹé,
  le fuaⓂaⓇ feaⓇtaine, Ⓓ'áⓇⓄuiᵹ ᵹaoⱦ.
Ⓓo ṁaⱦⱦnuiᵹ an ⱡⓇiú, 'ᵹuⓇ iⱤ uṁal Ⓓo ⱡaⓇaⓂaⓇ,
Aᵹ Ⓥéanaṁ an ⱡuain anuaⱤ ⱡum ⒹaiⓇbⓇe,
'ⓃuaiⓇ béiⱡ an feaⓇ ⱤⱦiúiⓇ, aⓇ mo Ɽuan Ⓓo ⱣⓇeabaⱤ-Ɽa;
  Ⓓo bioⱤ im' ⱡoⓂlaⓌ iⱤ ⒹúiⱤiᵹeaⓌ mé.

II

Cia ⱡíⱤeaⓌ an báⓌ aⱤ báiⓌ an ṁaiⓂean úⓌ,
  Sáⱦ' Ɽé maiⓂe uiⱤⱦe, iⱤ Ⓓo b'áⱤⓌ í a léim,
'ⓃuaiⱤ ⱤⱡaoileaⓂaⱤ cnáib aᵹuⱤ ᵹáⱤⓂaiⓌe Ɽáṁa uiⱤⱦe
  Ᵹaⱡ ⱡláⱤ aᵹ ⱡnaᵹaⓌ, aᵹuⱤ í aᵹ ⱤáⱤ maⱤ ⱣiléaⱤ!

Ⓓo ⱱeineaⱹaⱤ í ⱤⱦiúⱤaⓌ aⱤ ⱡúⱤⱤa ⱦaⱤⱤainᵹⱦe,
SⱣuⱦanna aᵹ bⱤúᵹaⓌ le Ɽiubal na hanaiⱤⱦe,
Ⓝí ⱤaiⓌ luaⱤⱡaⓌ aⱤ an lín ó'n mⒹaoi ᵹo Ⓓainᵹean ⱤiaⱤ,
  Ᵹo nⒹeaⱡamaiⱤ ᵹo CaⱤⱤaiᵹ ᵹlaⱤ áⱤⓌ na Ⓝaom.

III

Ⓥí CaⱤⱤaiᵹ lomáin maⱤ ⱡⱤáin aᵹ ⱤⱡⱤeaⓌaⓌ Ɽóṁainn,
  AⱤ ⱦí Ɽinn Ⓓ'alⱣaⓌ, le n-áⱤ ⒹⱦaoiⓌ ⱡlé;
Ⓥealaⱡ na n-éiᵹ Ⓓo ᵹéim maⱤ ⱦaⱤⓋ Ɽóṁainn,
  IⱤ ⒹaⱤ nⒹóiᵹ níoⱤ ⱦaiⱤe Ⓓo'n ꝽeaⱣánaiᵹ éiᵹeaṁ
CéaⓌ molaⓌ le hÍoⱤa CⱤíoⱤⱦ náⱤ caillea ⒹⱤinn!
IⱤ ná fuaiⱤⱦeaⱤ Ɽinn Ɽinⱦe i nⒹuiⱱeaᵹán faiⱤⱤᵹé,
Aⱡⱦ Ɽanam' aⱤiⱤ ᵹo ⒹⱦiᵹiⓌ an ⱡalma,
  AᵹuⱤ Ɽaⱡam Ⓓo'n ⱡaⱤⱤaiᵹ le conᵹnaṁ Ⓓé.

IV

Do bí an tAtair Diarmuid 30 dian a3 a3airt
    Ar Ríg na nAin3eal an cníú teact raor,
A3ur do cualatar ruar é i n-uactar Paratair.
    'Nuair adubairt an paidir ór ár 3cionn 30 léir.
Do 3lanamair poinnte Rinn' 3il' Catrac,
Bí an 3óilín ríor 30 mín, tair, calma,
Níor rtadamair de'n rcríb 30 ndeacamair do'n Calat.
    Ir d'ólamair fleagan 'dtí3 Seain Mic Aoda.

V

Bí an fuireann úd ruar tar éir uamain na fairr3e,
    'Nuair do b'fonn leir an ra3art an cníú do téad
Do tó3 ré leir ruar iad 30 cuan an maiteara,
    Ar bruac an tea3lai3 úd Seain Mic Aoda.
D'fanamair annrúd a3 diú3ad an baraille,
Mar a raib fairrin3 de'n lionn le fonn d'a rcaip-
        ead a3ainn ;
Sinn a3 faire ar 3ac uair 30 h-uair na maidne,
    A3ur an uamain 3ur fearaim 30 fáinne an lae.

VI

Ir deacair an bád do cáinead, 3eallaim díb,
Le 3nárta an Atair-Mic táini3 raor,
Tu3 an fuireann úd rlán ó Báid na Scealg
    An lá bí anfad árd 'ran aer.
Ca bfuil an t-ártac le fa3áil do b'fearra
Do 3earrfad carán tré lár na mara ?
Dá bearcaib rin táim-re fá3aint barra
    A3 an mbáidín 3reannta rin Seain Uí Néill !

23

Another tale of an eventful Skellig visit is the story of Ana Ní Áine — the old woman of Kenmare. Freely translated from *Scéalta ón mBlascaod,* it runs like this:

"When I was a young woman my father had a pleasure boat and many strangers would come to our house to sail from place to place with him. One fine Autumn day myself and another girl decided to accompany them to the Skellig; there was also a young priest in the boat with us.

"We set out for Skellig but before we reached the island a dreadful darkness approached from the West. My father wanted to put the boat about and head for home, but the others would not hear of this.

"The dark cloud steadily approached with great gusts of wind. The priest looked towards it. 'There is some mystery in that cloud', he said.

"It was now bearing down on us until it was almost upon the boat, and then we could see that within the cloud was the spirit of a woman!

"The priest jumped to his feet, put his confessional stole around his neck and took his book in his hands. He spoke to the woman and asked her what caused her unrest.

'I killed a person' said the woman.

'That's not what damned you' said the priest.

'I killed two people' said the woman.

'It's not that either' said the priest.

'I killed my own unbaptised child — whose father was a priest', said the woman.

'That indeed is the cause of your damnation' said the priest. "Then he began to read from his book and in a short moment the released spirit rose in a great flash and disappeared from sight".

The storyteller concludes: "We didn't continue to the Skellig that day; we returned home".

Surprisingly, one cannot find many such tales of the supernatural in relation to Skellig. Maxwell's *A Book of Islands* leaves one such situation hanging in mid air:

"Everything was so peaceful that I climbed down to a concealed lighthouse on the island's outer flank to see if the night could be spent there. Meanwhile Tom pursued his archaeological study of the ruins.

"The lighthousemen gave no encouragement. Nobody, they said, was allowed to stay without permission from Trinity House in Dublin. Nor would anybody in his senses want to stay there. The island was haunted and things often thumped on their own bolted door at night while the banshees wailed from the graveyard.

"Surely, I suggested, this would be the shearwaters, but they replied with scorn that they knew all the birds as they had nothing else to study. It could be the monks with uneasy consciences, or it could be the poor souls whose lives they had been unable to save after a ship-

Puffins pose at the "Wailing Woman" in Skellig Michael. This stone is reputed to be one of the "Stations of the Cross" which once lined the pilgrims' route.

wreck a few years ago — or it could be something else.

"Tom was sitting on the ground looking pale and shaken when I returned. Before I could speak he said: 'For God's sake let's get off this island at once'. And then he added: 'Something nearly pushed me over the cliff when I was climbing to some nettles just below the oratory, and after I had got back to Christ's Saddle some force struck which threw me flat on my face'.

"Coming from so powerful and fearless a man as Tom this was extraordinary and, on top of what the lighthouseman had been saying, extremely sinister. Our descent to the boat was made with backward glances......"

Over the years the penitential nature of the early Skellig pilgrimages developed into something quite different. Foley puts it this way: "Generally, in the latter days of these pilgrimages, the religious ceremonies were attended almost exclusively by girls and bachelors who were considered duly eligible for marriage. Of course, the idea was to spend Holy Week in fasting and praying. However, it transpired that many of the young 'eligibles' instead of fasting and praying, visited the island with the intention of courting, dancing, drinking and enjoying themselves in other various amusements..."

Finally, not only were the annual pilgrimages denounced from the altar, but when the practice persisted the police got orders to clear the rock.

Possibly from these pilgrimages, possibly from the changes of the Gregorian calendar in 1782, or possibly because the early monastery Abbot had outranked the local Bishop, a peculiar custom evolved — a tradition that the annual ecclesiastical period of Lent arrived later to Skellig than it did on the mainland, and consequently that marriage could be contracted on the Skellig at times when this would be impossible on the mainland of Ireland. It is not known if anyone ever availed of this facility, but the "Skelligs Lists" — the annual, anonymous and highly defamatory poems of the era — suggested many possibilities:

And down in the cabin,
As Skellig draws near,
See Maggie so strongly caressed.
And Patsy McCann whispers
'Shortly, my dear,
We'll hold our heads high like the rest!

The Hegarty lad
From the Strand Street bohaun,
Is there with his Mary tonight.
The Abbot of Skellig
Will wed them at dawn —
A wedding that cannot be white...

"The sense of solitude, the vast heaven above and the sublime monotonous motion of the sea beneath..." Part of the monastery with Small Skellig behind.

Left – the final flight of steps from Christ's Saddle to the monastery plateau.

Of the many Skellig Lists retained in the Archives of the Department of Irish Folklore, U.C.D., the List of 1922 from Lispole, in the Dingle peninsula is unique insofar as it deals — in humorous fashion — more with the nautical difficulties of sailing to Skellig than with the characteristics of the couples involved.

This Skellig group is depicted as departing from Minard harbour, but there was only one small boat — and that was already full....

Then up stepped Thomas Moran when he saw his craft was gone,

Saying comrades dear and maidens fair, I have for you a plan.

If you'll agree and follow me, we'll sail for Skellig too

In a ship that's far more stately than a little mean canoe.

That barque lies over yonder we'll set afloat again,

And pack the holes up safely with bags of barley grain.

You need not be the least afraid; believe me when I say

She'll float as safe as Noah's Ark with you across the main.

Away we went with one consent to where "Ruthickman" lay,

And soon we had her floating on the waters of the bay.

The passengers, they went on deck, and all prepared to go.

'Twas then they found they had no sails,

Which filled their hearts with woe.

"Don't worry boys," said Moran, "the ladies' shawls will do".

He asked them and he got them — without a grumble too.

They tied them up along the masts, and when they caught the wind,

'Twas quick and soon they sailed away, and left Minard behind.

Skellig Lists such as these, some of them containing up to forty verses — humorous, satirical, vicious — were common throughout Munster from Dingle to Cork for at least the past 140 years, but perhaps it is just as well that the custom has died out recently, or libel actions would be widespread.

This letter, received by a Cork printer in 1834, must be typical of the irate feelings of Skelligs List victims.

Sir, You are requested to take notice that I will hold you responsible for any liberties taken with the names of Mary Ellen Harris, Sarah Harris and Eliza Driscoll, they being members of my family, and having received intelligence of some person or persons wishing to expose them in the Skelligs Lists which are to come to and through your press, I am determined to indict all persons concerned if there is anything prejudicial to their person, interest or character in any manner.

Hugh Driscoll,
January 28, 1834.

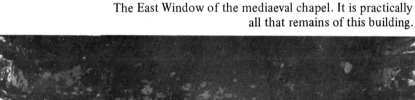

The East Window of the mediaeval chapel. It is practically all that remains of this building.

The Sea Journey

he modern Skellig 'pilgrim' might well assume that all the ancient problems of access to the island have been eliminated in this age of sturdy, seaworthy, diesel-engined fishing boats; but he would be wrong! True, the modern local fishing boat is far removed from the hide-covered craft of old, and true, it would be quite possible nowadays to beat a reasonable passage to Skellig through most weather — fog, calm or Force 6 — but irrespective of the mode, comfort or difficulty of the sea journey from the mainland, it is the sea condition immediately around the small, exposed landing of Skellig Michael which dictates access to the island.

Of course it is never necessary to travel all the way to Skellig to assess the landing conditions; all the local, mainland boatmen have a yardstick closer to home which will give them a very accurate appraisal of the possibilities. A Valentia man, for instance, can look at the "Holy Ground" rocks — 16 miles from Skellig — and decide on that observation if a landing is feasible. A Derrynane man may take one look at "The Pigs" outside his own harbour and base his decision on the conditions there. This is something which frequently baffles the visitor. On what appears to be a perfect summer's day, no boatman will take a Skellig party to sea!

So you must sit and wait for tomorrow. And ponder that this inaccessibility — in an age when we have access to the moon — is all part of the powerful magnetism of Skellig — the enhanced attraction of the unattainable!

Winter is out of the question. Even a whole week without wind in the period November to March — an unlikely occurrence at best —

Above — The modern Irish lighthouse tender, *Gránuaile*, steaming out of Valentia harbour.

Below — On the horizon 8½ miles South-west of Valentia, the Skelligs. Small Skellig left, and Skellig Michael right.

would hardly be sufficient to calm the ocean around Skellig. During this season, Skellig cliffs are sea-lashed from every side. Great long swells, which may have travelled 500 miles from some distant depression, mingle with local gales to create a terrible fury in which Skellig landing is scarcely visible. Winter wave crests will break 30 ft. high over the pier and reach 200 ft. up along the lighthouse road. The receding turmoil of every wave-trough will expose ragged seaweed stumps, sponges and anemones on the rock faces which are normally 10 metres below the mean surface. And this is the sheltered side of the island!

From April onwards, conditions can be expected to improve, and on fine summer days, fishing boats from Valentia, Cahirciveen, Portmagee and Derrynane frequently provide a service for visitors to Skellig. The traveller of 80 years ago could hire a rowing boat and four oarsmen exclusively for a Skellig trip at 25 sh. (£1.25) a day. In the economics of today's (1975) motorboats, the price range is still good value: £3.00 per seat, return, or approximately £30.00 for a day's exclusive hire of a £10,000 boat with capacity, safety and comfort for 12 passengers.

It is 10.45 a.m. on a fine summer's morning at Knightstown harbour, Valentia Island. The Shannon/Fastnet weather forecast — "South-west 2/3; Visibility 25 miles; 1040 millibars; Steady-" indicates a good day for Skellig, and one of the local boats is preparing to make the trip. Half-a-dozen passengers step on board, with lunch boxes well packed for a full day's outing, and a selection of sweaters and rain coats — "just in case"! They are foreign tourists and this is typical. Relatively few local Irish people visit Skellig, while foreigners of many nations can speak with authority and enthusiasm on all our National monuments and Natural history.

"Cast off"! We have a brief stop at nearby Renard Point pier to pick up two more passengers and then we set off Southwards through the five-mile corridor of Valentia harbour. On either hand, pebble beaches slope up to green field, yellow bog and blue mountain as we head for Portmagee, our final pick-up point before the open sea.

Kindred spirits on board recognise one another instantly across barriers of language, race and age in the spontaneous comaradarie of a shared shipboard adventure. Binoculars are compared with interest and the merits of German, Japanese and Russian brand-names are extolled. At least there is concensus on one point: "7 x 50" is the most suitable for boat-work where motion must be considered. Cameras, similarly, are much in evidence from the Hasselblad to the 'Box Brownie'. They may vary in quality and operation but the end products are very similar: memories of a certain summer's day.

Some diving Black guillemots, (Cepphus grylle), red-legged, black-

A winter storm roars around Skellig, sending spray hurtling
to the lighthouse — and higher

beaked, and really as much white as black in appearance, occupy our attention. They spend their lives — summer and winter — here in the sheltered shallows of the bay and seldom venture out to the open sea. Yet, of all the seabirds, their nests are the most difficult to find.

One-legged at the water's edge on Reen-a-Rea point stands a forlorn heron, (Ardea cinerea), grey and sombre. Hump-backed, he waits for low water to go fishing. The wash from our passing boat slope about his knee, but it doesn't bother him.

Valentia bridge and Portmagee village are reached and soon left behind. Our channel widens, and Valentia's Bray head, one of the Western extremities of the Irish coast, towers high on our right hand. On the left, we round Horse island, local home of the Lesser black-back gull, (Larus fuscus), and at last we catch our first glimpse of Skellig, directly ahead and 8½ miles away. This is the transition point between harbour and ocean and we feel the first gentle touch of the Atlantic in one of her kinder moods. Our course is 225º (C.), speed 7½ knots; destination: 51º 46' 20" N. 10º 32' 58" W., E.T.A. 12.55, local time!

One of the younger passengers wonders if he may steer the boat for a while? And indeed he may. In these fine conditions the skipper is only too happy to hand over the wheel temporarily and take the opportunity to chat with the other passengers.

The vast panorama of the open sea expands around us as we forge ahead: the Blasket islands, 15 miles away to the North, a wide, empty horizon to the West, the two Skelligs and the Lemon rock to the South-West, Puffin island, Bull rock and more miles of endless ocean to the South, and astern of us, the old red sandstone fingertips of Kerry's Macgillycuddy Reeks digging their nails into the sea. Out here we meet the oceanic seabirds, guillemots, puffins, razorbills.... swimming, flying, diving and making their living in various ways. An alarmed puffin surfaces too near the boat and amuses everyone by trying to take off in a panic and making a fiasco of it! He changes his mind and dives again to safety. To the West, flocks of noisy kittiwakes are vigorously working a shoal of sprats, and farther on the black, triangular dorsal fin of a basking shark, (Cetorhinus maximus), protrudes 3 ft. above the surface of the sea. This remarkable giant — which may be as long as our boat — wanders slowly about the tide-streams, his awesome, gaping white mouth doing nothing more sinister than collecting microscopic plankton! If we take the boat too near, he simply slides down out of sight for a few moments and returns to his meal of surface plankton when all is clear.

The first gannet — a reconnaissance outrider from Small Skellig — flies overhead on the ceremonial circuit of inspection. He is followed by others and still more, and as we approach the island a thousand

Barrels of fuel for the lighthouse generators are landed in very calm weather. The derrick lifts them directly from the supply boats at Cross Cove.

gannets are in the air around us. Another thousand — it would appear — occupy every visible ledge on Small Skellig, and as many more are plummeting like guided missiles into a fish shoal on the Northern side of the island. Where can you better this incredible experience? Possibly one place in the world! Only St. Kilda in the Outer Hebrides can boast more gannets than Small Skellig.

"Regardez le phoque"! "Kijk naar de zeehonden"! "Féach an rón glas"! "Seals! Seals! There on the rocks"! Pointing fingers are outstretched in a jumble of excited languages and the cameras are re-trained and re-focussed and re-shot — and ultimately re-loaded with feverish haste.

Eventually Skellig Michael — our final goal — looms high above us, solid, massive, awe-inspiring, its sheer cliffs leading all the way to heaven. We throttle back and slip in longside the tiny pier where one of the lighthouse men is waiting to lend a hand. Our lines are made fast. The engine is stopped. It is 12.55 p.m. and a modern pilgrimage to Skellig has begun!

The calmest day of 1973 at the small exposed landing of Skellig Michael. In fine weather, fishing boats from Valentia, Cahirciveen, Portmagee and Derrynane visit the island. Details of such trips are available at all local hotels and guesthouses.

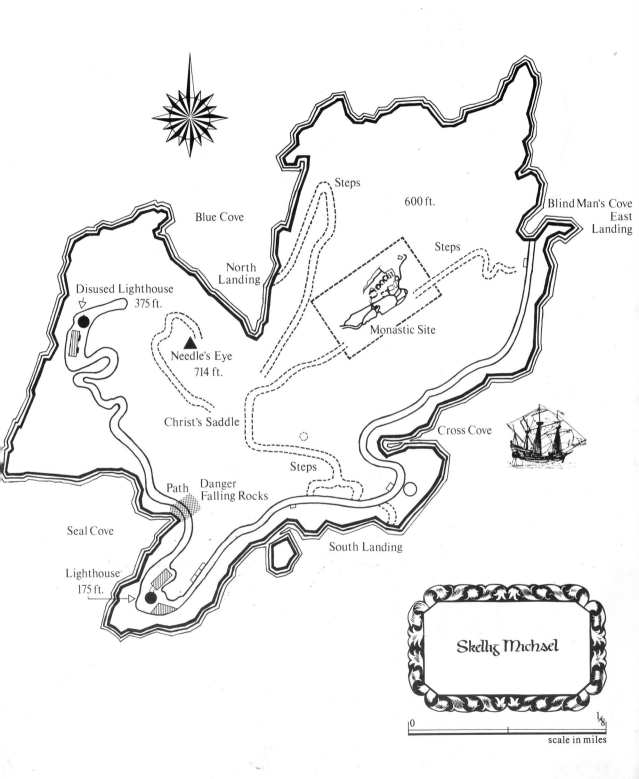

Steps

600 ft.

Blue Cove

Blind Man's Cove
East
Landing

North
Landing

Steps

Disused Lighthouse
375 ft.

Monastic Site

▲ Needle's Eye
714 ft.

Christ's Saddle

Cross Cove

Steps

Path Danger
Falling Rocks

Seal Cove

Lighthouse
175 ft.

South Landing

Skellig Michael

0   1/8
scale in miles

37

Up to the Monastery

The lands of the mainland monastery at Ballin-skelligs were disposed of in the 16th century, and included in the lease to Gyles Clinsher in 1578 was "a small island called Skellig Michell..." Later, the island which certainly was uninhabited by that time, passed to John Butler of Waterville for rental of "two hawks and a quantity of puffin feathers yearly". About 1820, the body which is now the Commissioners of Irish Lights bought the island for the purpose of erecting a lighthouse. In 1871, shortly before the Offices of Public Works took over responsibility for the maintenance of the monastic site, Lord Dunraven produced the first detailed archaeological account of Skellig Michael, describing the whole monastic establishment rather as it still is today — a main enclosure of old stone dwellings and oratories, with some associated outbuildings, terraces and pathways throughout the island. Certain renovations to the monastic site have been attributed to "the lighthouse workmen who... in 1838, built some objectionable modern walls". Another report of 1892 says: "We cannot conclude this account without protesting strongly against the way in which repairs are being carried on at Skellig Michael by the Board of Works.

"At the time of the visit of the Cambrian and Irish archaeologists an ordinary mason was seen calmly tinkering away at the ruins, pulling down a bit here and building up a bit there in imitation of the old style of work, without any kind of superintendence whatever. The vandalism perpetrated some time ago by the same authorities, at Inishmurray, is being repeated here with a vengeance".

Were these outbursts justified — or was the wording a little too

The entrance to the
monastery enclosure.

"The Priest's Stone",
standing in the "Monks
graveyard", within the
monastic enclosure, this is
the most impressive slab
on the island.

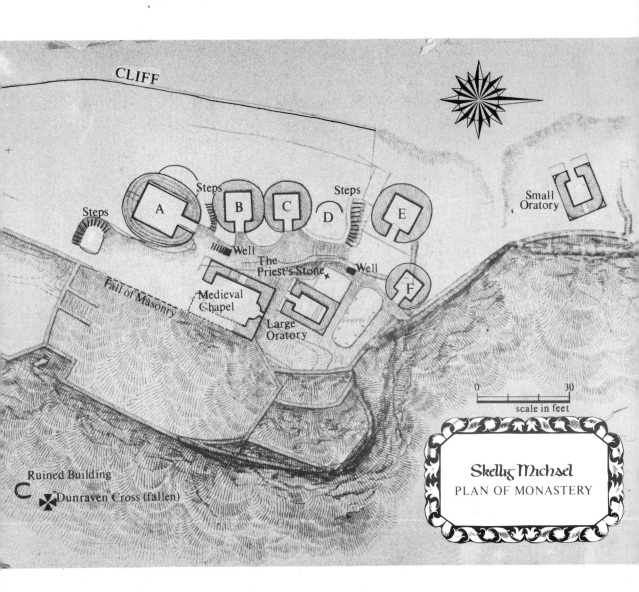

CLIFF

Steps

A

Steps

B

C

D

Steps

E

Small
Oratory

Steps

Well

The
Priest's Stone

Well

F

Fall of Masonry

Medieval
Chapel

Large
Oratory

Ruined Building

C

Dunraven Cross (fallen)

0   30
scale in feet

Skellig Michael
PLAN OF MONASTERY

40

Above — An aerial view of Skellig monastery from the North-East. Current access route is by means of the pathway entering the enclosure near the upper left-hand corner of the photograph.

Opposite page —This plan of the Skellig monastery is based on the plan from Lord Dunraven's *Notes on Irish Architecture* but the author has added additional detail and used a different code for the dwellings.

strong? In any event, one accepts today that Skellig is largely the genuine handwork of the monks dating from some 1400 years ago.

There are three ancient access paths cut and built into the rock faces from sea level up to the monastery, 600 ft. above. The direct and steep Eastern climb from Blind Man's cove, the Southern, part modern, zig zag path from Cross Cove, and the steep Northern path from Blue Cove which joins the Southern route at Christ's Saddle, 400 ft. above the sea.

The Eastern climb leads up very steeply on the sheer face immediately above the landing. Parts of it have fallen away and become overgrown, but the principal reason why it is not used — or even seen today — is because the lighthouse road-builders of 1820 blew away all the lower approaches to this route. The path is accessible now only by mounting a steel ladder (part of some lighthouse service equipment) on the roadside about 300 ft. from the landing. From the top of this ladder a careful traverse to the North brings one safely onto the old stairway.

And what a beautiful route this is, with much more interesting stonework than the other climbs. Near the top of this path, before it reaches the monastery enclosure, is the island's third "well" which has not been mentioned by any of the early chroniclers. Here also, rediscovered in 1974, is a large stone cross which was depicted by Dunraven in 1871, but lost to the intervening generations.

The Northern climb from Blue Cove is not nearly so steep and although it too is overgrown and dilapidated in patches, it is quite passable. At the bottom of this route, a section of about 150 ft. has been enlarged by explosives — probably during the 1820 period of lighthouse construction.

Under today's prevailing weather a boat could use this North landing perhaps only four days a year, so the very fact that the monks undertook the giant task of constructing the stairway to this bleak cove is a good argument that weather conditions then were far removed from those obtained now.

The South landing, by comparison, is quite useful and its lower steps below the roadway have been used and improved by the lighthouse authorities from time to time. But there is some mystery here too: Carved into the solid rock face nearby are fourteen steps which are virtually inaccessible, stopping short at both ends and leading neither to the sea nor the higher levels!

To reach the monastery today, one normally follows the lighthouse road from the landing point at Blind Man's Cove to a junction just beyond Cross Cove where the real ascent to the monastery begins via the old Southern stairway of some 600 steps.

Access to the monastery terrace is by a tunnel in the retaining

Above – Part of the Eastern climb to the monastery. This is the site depicted by Dunraven in 1875. Small Skellig is seen behind.

Top left – The Dunraven cross of 1875. It was unearthed in 1974, having been lost for many years.

Below left – Engraving from Dunraven's *Notes on Irish Architecture* 1875. This beautiful cross had fallen, broken in two and become completely overgrown until its re-discovery in 1974. Dunraven's impression of the site is rather elaborate and misleading; the true situation is shown in photo above.

Above — Detail from the roof of Cell "A".
It is thought that the protruding stones were
used as anchorages to secure protective sods
or thatch

Opposite page — Fourteen steps to nowhere.
Virtually inaccessible, these steps are carved
from the solid rock, but they lead neither to
the sea, nor the upper levels.

Above — Cell "A" on the left; the East window of the ruined mediaeval chapel to the right, with the modern gravestone conspicuous in front of the window. This is the general view upon entry to the final enclosure. It is interesting to compare this photograph with the Dunraven view on the page opposite taken in 1871.

Opposite page — Old photograph of monastic enclosure taken during repair work in 1871.

wall, and upon emerging within the shelter of this enclosure — some 300 ft. x 100 ft. — one finds the old stone dwellings and oratories huddled close together at various levels, almost as perfect as they were on the first day .

"The scene is one so solemn and so sad", says Dunraven, "that none should enter here but the pilgrim and the penitent. The sense of solitude, the vast heaven above and the sublime monotonous motion of the sea beneath would oppress the spirit, were not that spirit brought into harmony..."

There are six corbelled, beehive-shaped huts and two boat-shaped oratories as well as many stone crosses and slabs, some graves, two wells — said to "become dry in the case of cursing, swearing or blasphemy" — and the ruin of the mediaeval church. Tradition tells that there is also a deep subterranean tunnel leading away from the monastic site but although there are two features in the enclosure which could be associated with this idea, there is no clear evidence of any tunnel as such today.

The monastery huts are more or less rectangular in plan at floor level and take on a circular shape as the corbelling progresses upwards. Taking them in the order in which one meets them:

Cell A has a floor area of 15' x 12' 6" and a height of 16' 6". The internal walls are almost straight to a height of 6' before the dome begins to narrow, and all around the interior of the walls at about 6' or 8' are protruding stone pegs which may have supported a wooden 'upstairs' floor. The windows high up in the East and West walls would have given light at this level. On the exterior of the hut other stone pegs protrude and these may have been anchorages for protective sods or thatch. The door is 4' x 2' 9" and the walls are 6' thick.

Cell B is 9' x 9' and 10' high. There are two "cupboard" recesses in the internal walls, but there are no windows or no protruding pegs inside or out. The door is 4' 4" x 2' and the walls are 3' 6" thick at the door.

Cell C is 9' x 8' 6" x 11'. It is quite like Cell B without windows or protruding stones. The door is also the same size.

Cell D is only a ruin which may have been circular in plan. Its collapse is not of recent times.

Cell E is very similar to Cell A. It also has the internal stone pegs on the walls. The floor, which is very well laid is 12' x 11' 9" and the height is 13'. The door is 4' 6" x 3' and the walls are 4' thick.

Cell F — It is thought that the roof of this cell collapsed between 1871/1891, and that the dome was reconstructed inaccurately, some 3' less than its previous height. This cell is now 8' 2" x 9' x 10'. There are three "cupboard" recesses in the internal walls and again the internal stone pegs. The door is 3' 10" x 2' and the walls are 3' 6" thick at the

This square-shaped tower in the outer garden raises questions. What date and what purpose? Cell A is seen in the background.

Above – Cell C, it has no windows and the typical small entrance measures 4' 4" x 2'.

Opposite page – The Small Oratory. Note that it is built on reclaimed ground which is supported by a substantial artificial terrace.

Above — The grave of the lighthouse children who died in 1868 and 1869. This monument was erected some time later than 1871, as it does not appear in the Dunraven photograph on page 46.

Opposite page — This watercolour by T. N. Deane R.H.A. shows the old lower lighthouse. This building was demolished in 1966 and replaced by the present modern lighthouse.

door.

Large Oratory — This building is boat-shaped with a door in the Western wall. Its measurements are 12' x 8' x 10'. The altar across the Eastern wall is not likely to be very old as it contains some bricks which date to 1820 or later. There is a small window above the altar in the Eastern wall.

Small Oratory — This building is on a substantial artificial terrace some distance away from the group. It is 8' x 6' x 8' and there is a window, 2' x 11" in the North-Eastern wall. The door is only 3' x 1' 9" and the walls are 3' 2" thick.

Mediaeval Church — This is quite a ruin but its Eastern window still stands. In the centre of the church is a comparatively modern gravestone which refers to the lighthouse families of 1868, and was erected in this position some time after 1871.

The Lighthouse
and its Men

rior to 1820 there was no lighthouse between Cape Clear, County Cork, and Loop Head, on the Shannon — some 111 miles, as the gull flies, — of Ireland's fiercest coast. That was the year when, on request of Sir Maurice Fitzgerald, Knight of Kerry, approval for a lighthouse on Skellig Michael was granted. The Corporation for Preserving and Improving the Port of Dublin — predecessors of today's Commissioners of Irish Lights — bought the island from Butler of Waterville for the sum of £800, and Engineer George Halpin was given a formidable construction task:

To distinguish Skellig Michael from Loop Head or Cape Clear, and to ensure a wide arc of visibility, the plan called for two lighthouses on the rock — one at 175 ft. above sea level near Seal Cove, and the other at 375 ft. above sea level on the island's Western extremity. As well as this, some 3,200 ft. of approach road had to be built from the landing place at Blind Man's Cove right out to the upper lighthouse at the opposite end of the rock, and clinging to the cliff face every inch of the way.

Desirable though this project was, some writers of the period were greatly alarmed by one aspect of the construction work. Butler, in his sale, had stipulated that the monastery buildings be carefully preserved, but it transpired that the road builders and lighthouse builders had been living in some of the monastery cells and using others for storing explosives. However, by 1826, the two lighthouses were established — each showing a steady light and each having two semi-detached houses close by — where the keepers and their wives and families resided for long periods of duty. Writing in 1837, Samuel Lewis reported:

"The erection of the lighthouses has been a means of preventing

Above — framed in a disused doorway, the derelict old upper lighthouse which has been disused since 1866.

Left — engineer George Halpin's lighthouse road of 1820 — "clinging to the cliff face every inch of the way".

much loss of life and property. Scarcely a winter previously elapsed without frequent and fatal shipwrecks..."

One of the fatal Skellig shipwrecks to be recorded was the wreck of the *Lady Nelson*. Bound from Oporto to London with a cargo of wine and fruit, she struck the Skellig and went to pieces with the loss of all but three lives.

"The mate had warned the captain during the evening of his proximity to this dangerous rock; but the captain, who was drunken and jealous, (his wife having seconded the representations of the mate), refused to put the vessel about and in a couple of hours she struck".

"The mate and three hands saved themselves upon a part of the wreck, which was drifting about for two or three days, during which time they subsisted on the oranges and other fruit which, when the ship went to pieces, covered the sea around them. The mate, who was an excellent swimmer, procured these oranges by plunging off the spar and bringing them to his companions. On the third day, one man became delirious; saying that he should go ashore to dine, he threw himself off the spar and sank".

"Shortly afterwards the survivors were picked up by a fishing boat belonging to Dingle, which had come out looking for a wreck. The crew consisted of a father and his four sons, and had two pipes of wine in tow when they perceived the sufferers; finding their progress impeded by the casks and that the tide was sweeping the seamen into the breakers, where they must have been dashed to pieces, the old man nobly cut the tow line, abandoning what must have been a fortune to his family, and by great exertion picked the men up, just when the delay of a second would have caused their destruction".

"The *Lady Nelson port* is still famous in Kerry, and a glass of it is sometimes offered as a "bon bouche".

I have been quoting Chatterton, 1839.

What was life like at the Skellig lighthouses in those pioneer days? Perhaps there were good times but it is generally the hardship that is most-remembered. Hugh Redmond of Wexford, one of the first Skellig lighthouse crew, lost both his sons and his nephew over the cliffs. John Sloane, writing in 1873, recorded in some detail that another of the early Skellig lighthouse men arrived there — and departed — in very unhappy circumstances indeed. Michael Wishart had been Principal Keeper on the Tuskar Rock lighthouse in 1820, when he and his assistant, Charles Hunter, became involved in a substantial smuggling enterprise.

"....A large cask and several small kegs of brandy up to 84 proof.... and other excisable commodities". Not only were they storing the goods on the Tuskar, but they made the mistake of sampling them so heavily that they were unable to light the lantern — which, of course,

A souterrain? Is this opening, which now extends only six feet or so, associated with the legendary underground passage?

provoked deep inquiry. "I gained the tower on entering it, found Hunter dead drunk on his back and Wishart in the same state on his side, they having Tapped the Admiral".

On 23rd October, 1821, Michael Wishart was demoted from his post of Principal at Tuskar and sent to Skellig as Assistant, where he was killed by falling over the cliff while cutting grass for his cow.

It is easy to visualise such an accident on the steep slopes of Skellig. Even a century later Thomas Mason wrote:

"The Lighthouse keepers have a couple of goats which are generally located in some almost inaccessible position at milking time. With bated breath I have watched the men retrieve these perverse animals.... there is no place in the scheme of nature for a giddy goat..."

But at least, it couldn't happen today because there are no goats, and certainly no cows on the rock at present.

In or about 1870, Thomas McKenna of Crookhaven was dismissed from his post at Skellig lighthouse for being absent from duty when the "Commissioners" made a surprise visit. But where had he been? McKenna had gone exploring an underground tunnel in the monastery site but he ran into difficulty and was unable to get out. Eventually when his plight was discovered, one of his companions also entered the tunnel with a rope and brought McKenna to safety — but not before the "Commissioners" had appeared on the scene, made their feelings known and ordered that the entrance to the tunnel be closed... What was it? Where is it? What could it have held? Was this the underground tunnel of the earlier legend?

Detail from the prisms and lenses which are
the heart of Skellig lighthouse.

Another place with a story which is lost today because of rock-falls in the area is "Eliza's Corner" — a spot on the roadway between the two lighthouses which was named by Portmagee tradesmen who were working on the rock over 100 years ago. Eliza Callaghan, after whom the place was called, was a beautiful young woman who used to sit out at this corner for hours on end knitting in the sunshine. But was she a lighthouse daughter, much admired by the Portmagee men, or was she the mourning mother of the two children, Patrick and William Callaghan, who died in 1868 and 1869, aged two and three years, and who are buried in the mediaeval church ruin in the monastery? This is something I may never know.

That another family with young children occupied the Skellig lighthouse about twenty years later is known for certain however, because the late Mrs. Cahill of Portmagee — formerly Miss Joanie O'Sullivan — often recalled spending three years of her youth on Skellig Michael as teacher to the lighthouse children.

Soon after this period the decision was taken to move the light-house families to the mainland, and accommodation was rented in Valentia for this purpose for a number of years. Finally, about 1900, official dwellings were built at Valentia for Skellig lighthouse families and a system of relieving the keepers on a regular basis was introduced. Thus, Knightstown village took over from Portmagee which had been the Skellig shore-base since 1820.

The upper Skellig light was discontinued in 1866, and the lower light was altered to have a flashing character — which is still the means of distinguishing one lighthouse from another. In 1909 the latest type of paraffin vapour incandescent burner was installed as well as a new lens of dioptric type — that is to say, a lens made of a set of prisms placed around the light to focus into a horizontal beam.

This lens also holds the secret of the flashing effect. The whole optical assembly revolves around a steady light source at a fixed speed and gives the impression of a flash as the beam swings through the observer's point of view.

On Michaelmas Day, 1902 a Portmagee seine-boat which had been fishing by the Skellig was wrecked at the island's landing while the crew were ashore for a rest. The sudden wind which had done the damage also prevented help from coming for a week. Meanwhile, the Skellig larder had thirteen extra mouths to feed and the marooned fishermen had ample time to reflect on the tradition that nobody goes fishing on Michaelmas Day....

World War II brought its share of conflict to the Skellig area. Dogged aircraft encounters and bombing of merchant vessels were frequent occurrences, but neutrality and security maintained a blanket of silence on such events.

One of the few incidents to be recorded — 5th March, 1941 — was the loss of an unidentified aircraft which crashed into the sea south of Skellig. But even that tale ended abruptly, because a subsequent search by the Irish Lights tender and the Fenit lifeboat yielded only an empty rubber life-raft.

Explosive fog signals — four ounce charges, detonated electrically — were introduced at the Skellig in 1914. In 1936 Mason reported a gigantic explosion which occurred when an electrical fault detonated simultaneously some 300 of these explosive charges. "It nearly lifted the island out of the sea", but no harm ensued and this type of signal remained in use until 1953.

There was no fog at midnight on 18th November 1955 when the 90-ton French trawler, Styvel, ran headlong into the Skellig. She was heading home with a full cargo of fish when she hit the Northern side of the rocks where the lighthouse cannot be seen. Luckily there was no loss of life. Although the Styvel began to sink immediately, Valentia lifeboat managed to tow her from the 80-metre depths of the Skellig to the comparative safety of Valentia harbour before she finally went down.

Had the operation been a month later, the outcome might have been different because December 1955 saw some of the worst weather that the Skellig has ever recorded. On 27th December a wave broke the glass of the lighthouse lantern — 175 ft. above the sea — flooding the light and doing extensive damage. It was 3rd January, 1956 before a relief crew of fitters with new lighting equipment could be landed on the rock.

Bill Dumigan, now retired from the lighthouse service, recalls that Skellig accident:

"I was winding the light-machine when the lantern was smashed and I received a cut forehead from the broken glass... During the storm we also lost our boat-landing and cargo derrick; all the stanchions leading to the landing were bent and the road was ripped away".

And that year, which began with such difficulty was also to bring great tragedy to the lighthouse. On 22nd August 1956, keeper Seamus Rohu was reported missing from Skellig. His comrades and other helpers searched the island over and over again. Valentia lifeboat and the lighthouse service vessel, *Valonia,* searched the sea around the rock for days, but all in vain. It was a cruel blow.

By and large, the structure of the lower lighthouse remained as it was built in 1820 until quite recently. In 1964 the first step in a modernisation programme was taken with the installation of a powerful diesel derrick at Cross Cove, 140 ft. above the sea; this is used for landing hundreds of tons of building materials. 1965 saw the beginning of the reconstruction. The two old dwellings were made into one and all the old interior plaster walls were studded and lined with a decorative plastic finish. A bedroom was provided for each keeper and two spare bedrooms for visiting tradesmen. An office was included for the Principal Keeper. A new bathroom with H. & C. was installed and oil-fired central heating and electric power fitted throughout the building.

On 24th May 1966 a small temporary lantern with an electric flashing light was mounted on a nearby spur of rock, and the main light which had guided mariners for 146 years was extinguished. The old tower was swiftly demolished and shovelled into the sea, and in its place was erected a new reinforced concrete tower, engine room and battery room, a workshop and an oil pump room with a seven-year fuel supply. Instead of a paraffin vapour burner, a modern, three-kilowatt electric lamp was fitted, and the lens system of 1909 which was in perfect condition, was re-installed.

This new light, with its characteristic triple flash, its intensity of 1,800,000 candelas and its visible range of 27 miles came into operation on 25th May, 1967.

Today's Skellig lighthouse is a far cry from the original, not alone

Skellig's lower lighthouse was completely reconstructed in 1966. Meanwhile a temporary lantern (visible at the top of the photo) mounted on a nearby spur served mariners by night.

in construction, comfort and equipment, but also in transport, for instance. One remembers the industrious lighthouse relief boats — the 'old' *Ierne*, the *Deirdre*, the *Nabro*, the *Alexandra*, the *Valonia* and later the more sophisticated ships, the *Granuaile*, *Ierne*, *Isolda* and *Atlanta* — steaming around the coast on their lighthouse rounds.

One remembers the same ships weatherbound in harbour for days, perhaps weeks, while the Skellig men waited for relief and supplies. One remembers when emergency arose at these moments to complicate the situation, and the many mercy dashes which Valentia lifeboat made to the Skellig lighthouse to bring injured men to safety. The station files tell the exciting events — but briefly:

March 24th 1950: Lifeboat relieved Skelligs Rock. November 15th 1953: Assistant Keeper Gillian injured at Skellig. Landed by Valentia lifeboat. April 4th 1954, Captain Martin, Engineer of Irish Lights, ill on Skellig for seven days was taken ashore by Valentia lifeboat, after relief tender, *Valonia*, had failed to land in four attempts. June 15th 1963: Skellig keeper very ill. Taken off by Valentia lifeboat. October 25th 1965: Injured carpenter taken off Skellig by Valentia lifeboat....

All this is changed now. The Skellig dwellings on Valentia are closed. The lighthouse families live where they please, and the fortnightly helicopter service from Castletown flies the lighthouse keepers to and from the Skellig pad in a matter of minutes.

Lighthouse communications too have taken great strides. Since 1970 the men on Skellig can use the normal telephone which is linked by VHF beam with the mainland exchange in Castletown, and make their calls like any other subscriber. Before this they had only the shipping-band radio-telephone for communication with other lighthouse establishments or with shipping or, in emergency, with Valentia Radio Station.

But before that, before the advent of radio to Skellig? They had semaphore signals. There was a large white-washed patch on the rock-face beside the lighthouse road and a semaphore signaller standing in front of this could be read by telescope from the Bull Rock lighthouse — some 14 miles away — which, in turn, would relay the message ashore by similar means.

Two incidents highlight the difficulties of these early communications. In 1936, John Dore of Valentia, one of the three-man Skellig crew fell ill, but thick fog completely prohibited the normal semaphore communication with Bull Rock. Distress rockets were fired that night but of no avail. The fog persisted and the patient's condition grew worse.

The fog signal had to be manned by day. The light and the fog signal had to be maintained by night. Distress rockets had to be fired

The fortnightly helicopter, "Whiskey-Bravo", ferries relief keepers to and from Skellig lighthouse.

John Dore — brought safely ashore from the 1936 Skellig emergency.

Jim Lavelle. He built the Skellig bonfire in the emergency of 1936.

Patrick 'Bonnet' O'Shea, who came to the assistance of the Skellig lighthouse emergency in 1936.

regularly and a watch had to be kept for the possibility of help from a passing boat or the chance of a clearance and a contact with the Bull Rock.

A second night passed and the rockets were finally exhausted — without result. The patient was very ill, with only a basic first-aid box to succour him, and his two companions were still without sleep or even rest. What to do?

Every scrap of firewood, every box, packing case and provision basket, every newspaper, sack, rag and old uniform was carted manually, load by load, up the steep climb to the monastery pinnacle and a great bonfire was prepared. Oil from the lantern was drawn up the hill in gallons, tins, buckets and bottles and added to the fuel.

It was a whole day's work and as soon as darkness had fallen on the Skellig, Assistant Keeper Jim Lavelle set a match to his bonfire, sending flames roaring hundreds of feet into the air above the old monastery cells. The signal went far afield. A Portmagee fisherman, Patrick "Bonnet" O'Shea, who saw the glow in the sky, understood the message and brought help in time.

Thirty-six years previously, during the fishing season of 1900, a similar fire had brought help in a similar situation. This time the Cahills' six-oar "follower" set out from Valentia to answer the distress, and although most details of the successful rescue are forgotten, the sequel to it is still told in Portmagee and Valentia: When the rescue boat landed in Portmagee after its 20 mile dash, the Police Sergeant stood in the doorway of the Public House and refused to give the oarsmen admission because it was "off hours". Undaunted, they boarded their boat again and rowed the further five miles to Knightstown, where "Galvin" gave them the freedom of the house.

A puffin in flight seems to dwarf Small Skellig.

Sea Birds of Skellig

f there is one facet of the Skellig lighthouse-man's life which has not changed much in 150 years it is his interest in the lives and habits of nesting seabirds; and much of the ornithological literature of today received its early information from observant lighthouse men. Today, more than ever before, there is a growing appreciation of the Irish coast's wonderful natural treasure of birds — a treasure fast disappearing in other countries — and each year more and more students and observers are drawn here from far afield.

The Skellig rocks are Europe's ideal bird sanctuary. They are luckily situated far away from the pollution of city and industry, and Fate has been kind in forbidding such tanker disasters as the Torrey Canyon, which annihilated countless thousands of sea-birds in one area of England's South coast. Luckily too, the birds of Skellig — and there may be a quarter of a million of them — have never learned to fear man and on this rock one can study from a range of a few feet so many creatures which are never seen over the mainland.

The relative clumsiness of Skellig's seabirds, and the fact that they cannot take off from level ground but have to launch themselves from a ledge to become airborne, led to an early legend that some mysterious magnetism held the birds on the island. However, the terrestrial drawbacks are more than balanced by the great skill of the seabirds in the air and on — or beneath — the waves.

A well-matched pair of gannets, Small Skellig.

Gannet — *Sula Bassana*
Ir: *Gainéad*
Fr.: *Fou de bassan*
Ge: *Basstölpel*
Sw.: *Havssula*
Du: *Jan van Gent*

Pride of place in the bird life of the area must go to the gannet, which inhabits the Small Skellig rock to the relative exclusion of all other species. If there are some of the smaller sea-birds on the lower ledges it is only because these perches do not offer enough space for the heavy, goose-sized gannets. Every other site on this precipitous 16 acre, 445 ft. crag is taken up by the 20,000 nesting pairs, making Small Skellig the second largest of the world's 23 gannet colonies.

First mention of the Small Skellig gannetry was in 1700. In 1748 the gannet population was "an incredible number", and from then onwards the estimated figures fluctuated considerably.

1828 — 500 pairs
1880 — 30 pairs
1882 — 150 pairs
1906 — 15,000 pairs
1913 — 8,000 pairs
1941 — 10,000 pairs
1969 — 20,000 pairs

The gannet is obviously in a very strong position today, and one can only suggest that the fluctuations in the colony's early history were due to "harvesting". 150 years ago, gannets were fetching 1s. 8d. to 2s. 6d. each, and as late as 1869 the Small Skellig was rented annually for the taking of feathers and young gannets. At breeding time the rock was guarded by a boat-crew of twelve men, "well paid by the man who owned it", but this deterrent was inadequate, and Dunleavy — in O'Crohan's *The Islandman* — tells an exciting tale of one unauthorised gannet-raid which ended in bloodshed.

"This time a boat set out from Dunquin at night with eight men in her, my father among them, and they never rested till they got to the rock at daybreak. They sprang up it and fell to gathering the birds into the boat at full speed. And it was easy to collect a load of them for every single one of these young birds was as heavy as a fat goose. As they were turning the point of the rock to strike out into the bay, what should they see coming to meet them but the guard boat. They hadn't seen one another till that moment".

Then the activity began. The guards tried to take the Dunquin boatmen prisoners, but "...some of them sprang on board and they fell to hitting at one another with oars and hatchets, and any weapon they could find in the boat till they bled one another like a slaughtered ox".

Although outnumbered by twelve to eight the Dunquin men won the fight and eventually got back to their own harbour with their boat-load of gannets intact. When the vanquished guard boat reached its base, two men were dead, and the other ten were sent into hospital. "After that they were less keen on that sort of chase and the guard was taken off the rock...".

Even though the gannets do not lay until April or later, it seems that the nesting site is selected immediately on return from migration in February, and is guarded by one or other of the partners for the next six months. And this is hardly without reason. In a colony of 40,000 thieving neighbours any unattended property, be it site, materials, nest, egg or chick, is unlikely to survive very long.

Above — On Small Skellig, among the 20,000 pairs of nesting gannets, looking westward to Skellig Michael.

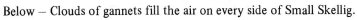

Below — Clouds of gannets fill the air on every side of Small Skellig.

The gannet makes a large, high nest of weeds and all sorts of floating rubbish, and only one dull, greenish, white egg is laid. When hatched, the chick is snow-white but its true feathers are first black and later mottled, and it is not until the fourth year that the full adult plumage is attained – pure white with bold black wingtips and yellow head. The mature gannet is 36" in length, with a long neck, long pointed bill, pointed tail and long narrow wings.

First-year gannets migrate in November to the West coast of Africa or even in to the Mediterranean, but in successive years they travel much shorter distances, the older birds reaching only as far as the Bay of Biscay. One record traveller – a young gannet ringed on Small Skellig in 1968 was subsequently recovered on the coast of Brazil!

The gannet's flight is usually direct and low with frequent gliding, but while feeding it wheels high in the air and will plunge into the sea upon its prey from 100 ft. or more. Evolution has designed the gannet well for this violent activity. It has no external nostrils, no real tongue, and has an intricate pneumatic system of air-cushion shock absorbers throughout its body.

The "Changing of the Guard" at the nest when the gannet returns from a fishing trip is a highly ceremonious show – which is not confined just to breeding time. Both birds stand face to face, wings half open, bowing to each other and knocking their bills together with much contented grunting. No doubt it could be a very graceful affair if they had enough space, but in the crowded conditions of the Small Skellig, any protruding wingtip or tail which encroaches by an inch on a niehgbour's territory is liable to provoke a sharp stab of retaliation which upsets the whole ceremony.

For two months the gannet chick remains in the nest, pampered and grossly overfed. Then it is deserted and it starves for two weeks before it plucks up the courage to take the plunge into the sea. If the young bird survives this first venture, it has a fair chance of living to an age of 40 years.

During his life the gannet will touch no other land locally but his breeding station, and there is only one report of a gannet ever fishing inland – in an Antrim lake on a stormy day in 1932.

The Small Skellig, which is owned by Mr. C. O'Connell of Dublin, has recently been leased by the Irish Wildbird Conservancy as an official seabird refuge, and studies still continue. On one July day in 1972, 671 young gannets were ringed and released.

Above — Modern fishing nets and twines made of buoyant synthetic fibres are put to good use as nesting materials by Skellig gannets.

Left — Every accessible ledge on Small Skellig is dotted with nesting gannets. Spacing is critical; any trespass on a neighbour's territory will provoke instant attack.

A puffin and two razorbills. Although they are neighbours, their nesting habits are quite distinct: The puffin nests in a burrow, while the razorbill lays its egg on a bare rock ledge.

Puffin — about to launch himself over the cliff. Most Skellig birds would be relatively helpless on level ground without the help of a slope for take-off.

Puffin — Fratercula arctica
Ir: *Puifín*
Fr: *Macareux moine*
Ge: *Papageitaucher*
Sw: *Lunnefågel*
Du: *Papegaaiduiker*

The puffin, like the razorbill and the guillemot, is one of the auk family — black and white salt water divers with short, narrow wings and legs set far back. Their carriage is upright and their flight is fast and whirring, seldom for long in a straight line. All these birds use their wings to swim underwater, and they have been seen by aqualung divers as deep as 15 metres.

On Skellig Michael the puffins breed colonially in rabbit burrows or similar holes from which the rightful owners may be forcibly ejected. Only one egg is laid, round in shape and whitish in colour with light

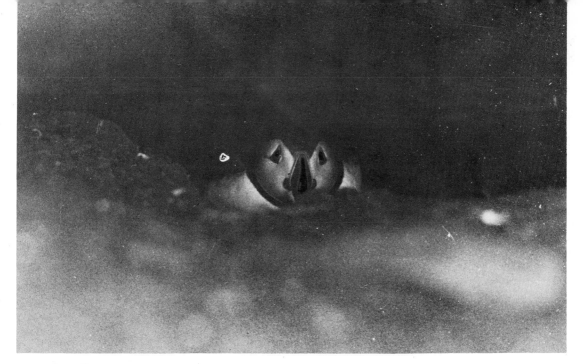

A puffin stares aggressively from its burrow. Puffins are fierce fighters and will easily evict a rabbit and take over the burrow.

grey/brown spots. When the puffin chick is six weeks old it is deserted by the parents to fend for itself and to make its own way to sea.

Up to the beginning of this century puffins were captured in great numbers. Their plumage was a valuable article of trade and the young birds, well salted, were regarded as a delicacy. Two salted puffins could fetch a "peck" of meal on the market.

The puffin is easily recognised: Black plumage above, white below, grey cheeks and bright orange feet, but the bill is the most conspicuous feature. In winter this is dull yellow, and small, but in summer it is bright red, blue and yellow, laterally flattened and very strong. In appearance the puffin, which is 12" in length, is stumpy and big-headed with an awkward shuffling gait. They are generally quiet birds, living from their underwater hunting, but when aroused or in a tussle over a nesting site they can fight fiercely.

When the flocks of puffins arrive back at Skellig at the end of March from their North Atlantic wanderings, they first swim around the rock for some days, not approaching very near. Then in the evening dusk a few — only a few — will venture ashore to spend the night. Finally in mid-April in the course of a couple of days the whole flock will settle on the island and take up residence. Skellig will now be over-run with puffins until the second week in August when, in response to some great unanimous decision, the puffins will depart as suddenly as they arrived.

Razorbill — Alca torda
Ir: *Crosán*
Fr: *Petit pingouin*
Ge: *Tordalk*
Sw: *Tordmule*
Du: *Alk*

The razorbill, 16" in length, is black above with white underparts. The bill is almost black in colour, laterally compressed and has a conspicuous white line across the centre. The razorbill has a heavier head and shorter, thicker neck than the guillemot. It also looks more squat while swimming and generally carries its tail cocked up.

From March to August the razorbills are on the Skellig, although some early-comers return at the end of January — and the ledges below the road at the lighthouse are well-populated nesting sites which can be observed without difficulty. One one egg is laid — a buff colour spotted with dark brown — and, unlike the puffin, the razorbill tends its young for a long period even after the nest has been abandoned. One conspicuous razorbill which retained its winter plumage in summer nested in the same spot on Skellig Michael for four years in succession.

Guillemot — Uria aalge
Ir: *Forach*
Fr: *Guillemot de troil*
Ge: *Trottellumme*
Sw: *Sillgrissla*
Du: *Zeekoet*

The guillemot is an inoffensive bird and its eggs and young are a constant target for gulls and other predators. Black or very dark brown above, white below, the guillemot is 16½" in length. A slender, more pointed bill and a thinner neck distinguish it from the razorbill.

The guillemot makes no nest, but lays its single egg in mid-May on some inaccessible, crowded ledge above Seal Cove. The egg varies very much in colour from brown to green or white, blotched and streaked with brown, but its distinct pear shape cannot be mistaken. This shape too prevents the egg from rolling off its unprotected ledge.

The kittiwakes build their nests on the sheer cliffs of Skellig Michael at Cross Cove.

Kittiwake — Rissa tridactyla
Ir: *Staidhséar*
Fr: *Mouette tridactyle*
Ge: *Dreizehenmöwe*
Sw: *Tretåig más*
Du: *Drieteenmeeuw*

On Skellig Michael the kittiwake is the noisiest bird. It nests on the ledges above the landing, and at Cross Cove and Seal Cove, and seems to spend its summer screaming madly at the world at large. The voice is loud and clear and cannot be mistaken: "kit-i-wake........ kit-i-wake"

The kittiwake is very much an open sea species which only once — in the year 1938 — has been seen inland. The wings and mantle are ash grey and the remainder of the plumage is pure white. It is distinguished from the common gull which is a similar size — 16" in length — by solid black triangular wingtips, olive/brown legs, an unmarked, yellow bill and a dark eye.

The kittiwake generally returns to the Skellig in March — although the lighthouse records for 1972 show that some kittiwakes returned as early as 26th December — and its three eggs — stone coloured, spotted with grey and brown — are laid at the end of May. The Kittiwake makes a sturdy nest of weeds and roots, and the largest Skellig Michael colonies are on the precipitous ledges of Cross Cove and Seal Cove — where the chicks are deserted to fend for themselves in August.

The infant mortality must be very high in these communities. Fights between adults on the narrow ledges frequently result in eggs or chicks being hurled over the edge and into the sea.

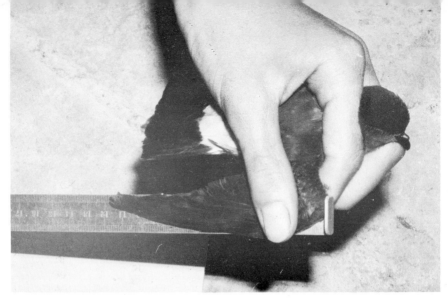

Bird studies: A storm petrel's wing measurements are taken and logged. Each bird is identified by a numbered ring on its leg and upon subsequent recapture, growth figures are obtained.

Storm petrel — Hydrobates pelagicus

Ir: *Mairtíneach*
Fr: *Pétrel tempête*
Ge: *Sturmschwalbe*
Sw: *Stormsvala*
Du: *Stormvogeltje*

At 6" in length, the storm petrel is the smallest European seabird, visiting land only while breeding. It is sooty black, with a conspicuous white rump and a square black tail.

There is a large breeding colony of storm petrels on Skellig Michael but they are seldom seen by day as they remain hidden in their nests or else far out to sea. At evening time they appear, flitting just above the waves, feet dangling so low that they appear to be running on the water.

They return to the Skellig at the end of April, and by the end of June one oval egg — white, with rust spots — is laid in a burrow, under a stone, or deep within the stonework of the old monastery buildings with little or no nesting material. Incubation takes 5 or 6 weeks and during this time the bird will often wander great distances for food, leaving the egg or the chick unattended for days.

Occasionally the voice of the storm petrel — a purring sound with a "hiccough" at the end — will lead you to its nest. But beware. This bird can spit out an evil-smelling oil with great accuracy if interfered with. The storm petrel, also known as "Mother Carey's Chicken" takes to the open sea again in October. They are never seen inland — except after some fierce storms in 1839 and 1891 when these birds were strewn dead over miles of countryside.

Manx shearwater — (Puffinus puffinus)
Ir: *Cánóg*
Fr: *Puffin des anglais*
Ge: *Schwarzschnabel — Sturmtaucher*
Sw: *Mindre lira*
Du: *Noordse Pijlstormvogel*

The manx shearwater is very clumsy on land and is seldom seen there by day. Even on fine, calm nights they prefer to hide away, and it is only on cloudy, windy nights when the shearwaters venture out in their full force and full voice, that an idea of the local population can be formed.

They are sometimes seen in groups, particularly towards evening time when large flocks gather on the water near the breeding ground. Sooty black above, white underneath and 14" in length, the shear-water is recognised easily by its distinctive flight — very low over the sea, following the contours of each wave, gliding frequently on stiff wings with only occasional wing beats.

In March the shearwaters return from their winter migration in South America. They breed in burrows and will use the same burrow year after year. One white, oval egg — very large in relation to the bird — is laid at the end of April and both birds sit, but frequently the nest is left unattended for days while the birds forage far afield for food.

In the summer of 1972 one shearwater had her nest at the foot of the altar steps in the old oratory of the Skellig monastery. Indifferent to visitors and cameras she sat for the prescribed time, but she must have moved to some more secluded site as soon as the chick arrived because from then on we saw her no more.

Parenthood is a long task for the shearwaters. Incubation takes 7½ weeks, and the chick remains in the nest for a further 10½ weeks, by which time it has become far heavier and fatter than the parent birds. Eventually it is deserted and suffers a week's starvation before it decides to venture forth to the sea. And this big initial adventure must be made under cover of darkness. The young shearwater is so helpless on land that it would be promptly devoured by gulls if it showed itself by day.

Fulmar — Fulmarus glacialis

Ir:
Fr: *Pétrel glacial*
Ge: *Eissturmvogel*
Sw: *Stormfågel*
Du: *Noordse Stormvogel*

Before the year 1900, the fulmar was a rare visitor to Ireland from Northern regions, but its numbers and breeding stations were rapidly spreading Southwards, and in 1913, R. M. Barrington reported 12 pairs nesting for the first time on Skellig Michael. Some 70 birds arrived in 1914, and about 100 in 1915. Thus the colony was established and from Skellig they spread out to other local rocks and cliffs.

The fulmar finally found peace in this period and this area. Only thirty years previously some 12,000 fulmars were "harvested" annually on St. Kilda alone — 115 birds per every member of the population. One report put it this way: "No bird is of such use. The fulmar supplies oil for their lamps, down for their beds, a delicacy for their tables, a balm for their wounds and a medicine for their distempers..."

The fulmar is gull-like in appearance, 18½" in length, with a white head and grey back, wings and tail. But here the similarity ends. The fulmar has a thick neck, a short, hooked, yellow bill with conspicuous tubed nostrils, and a distinctive, stiff-winged flight with wonderful mastery of air currents.

The fulmars are at Skellig from January to September. They nest at all levels, frequently in easily-accessible places among the tussocks of flowering "sea pink", both parents taking four-day duty tours incubating the single white egg which is enveloped completely in the underfeathers. Easily accessible, yes, but the fulmar will eject mouthfuls of foul-smelling oil at any curious intruder who comes too near.

Fulmars seen for the first time in a new area are not necessarily nesting; it is their habit to 'prospect' a cliff very thoroughly for a few seasons before deciding to breed there.

There are ravens on Skellig and there are hooded crows; there are choughs and rock pipits, oystercatchers and shags, herring gulls and black-backed gulls, all of which can also be found commonly on any nearby mainland cliff or beach. In spring and autumn, one can be lucky and sight many interesting migrating species from other regions — skuas, knots, great shearwaters, turnstones, phalaropes... but not one of these has quite the same magic as the island's truly oceanic natives, who live and die on the endless ocean, coming ashore here only of necessity to reproduce their own kind.

When the fulmar is hatching the egg is enveloped completely in her feathers.

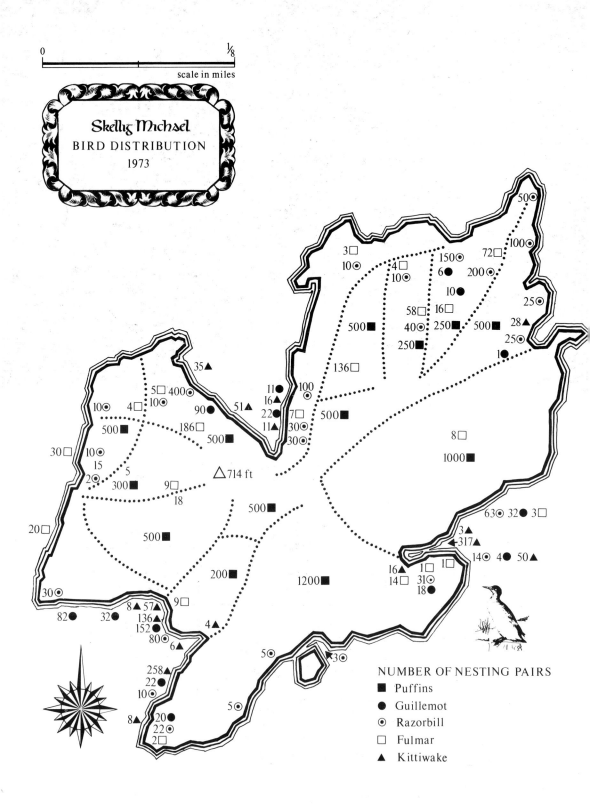

Skellig Michael

BIRD DISTRIBUTION

1973

0   ⅛

scale in miles

△714 ft

NUMBER OF NESTING PAIRS

■ Puffins

● Guillemot

⊙ Razorbill

□ Fulmar

▲ Kittiwake

Guillemots and kittiwakes on the lower ledges of Small Skellig.

Sea Birds of Skellig

Table of Numbers

	Skellig Michael		Small Skellig
Gannet	—		20,000 ('69)
Puffin	6,000/8,000	('69 & '73)	—
Razorbill	1,400	('73)	35 ('69)
Guillemot	200	('73)	575 ('69)
Kittiwake	950	('73)	1,120 ('69)
Storm Petrel	1,000/10,000	('69 & '73)	—
Manx Shearwater	1,000/10,000	('69 & '73)	—
Fulmar	588	('73)	10 ('69)

Geology and Plants

t is difficult to imagine that these isolated crags now surrounded by seas which are 80 metres deep, were once part of a great mainland peninsula — but this seems to be so. The 350 million year-old old red sandstone and green and purple slate of Skellig are identical to the adjacent mainland even in general direction and dip. Similarly too, a small number of fossil traces have been found, and to the North of Skellig's lower lighthouse, in an area of purple slate, are some calcareous patches which would merit more careful study in this respect.

Several major cracks or faults occur in Skellig Michael and these are particularly noticeable at sea level where they penetrate the rock as caves. All of these fissures have been entered and probed in recent years and while the caves at Blind Man's Cove and Cross Cove run for less than 150 ft., the openings under the lighthouse at Seal Cove, and under the North landing at Blue Cove are long interesting caverns which still hold most of their secrets.

Geology leads to botany and here a whole new aspect of Skellig opens up. Reading Crofton Croker's reports of a century-and-a-half ago, one must assume that he was not very accurate in his observations when he said: "Verdure there was none to soothe the eye of the weary pilgrim; all was nakedness and barren rock...." One can still generalise and say that the vegetation of Skellig is rather sparse, but this is not entirely true; there are thirty-eight species of hardy rock plants on Skellig Michael, which, in season, bloom from April onwards, providing patches of splendid greenery and colour.

All Skellig plants are rather common species — found in any sea-cliff terrain — and there is nothing which would relate directly to the

Sea-pinks, the light-headed, tough-rooted plants which hold much of the island's soil in place. In recent years these plants are dying mysteriously on large areas of the southern slope, and there is much consequent erosion.

earlier monastic cultivation. In legend only do we find reference to a miraculous crop of corn — and a miraculous supply of provisions which saved the monks from starvation until the corn could be harvested!

The most conspicuous — and puzzling — recent development in the flora of Skellig Michael is the fact that large areas of Sea pink are dying out. The whole southern face of the island which up to four years ago was a firm stronghold of the Sea Pink is now relatively barren and is overrun by swards of Rock sea spurrey. Botanists do not have an explanation for this, but far-reaching effects may well result from the change, because the tough root-systems of the Pinks were the main reinforcement for much of the soil on the island's steep slopes.

Small Skellig has not been extensively studied for plant life, and although very little greenery is evident to the casual observer, the eight species reported in the plant-lists may not really be the complete picture.

Plants of Skellig

Agrostis stolonifera	*Creeping bent*	*June-Aug.*
Agrostis tenuis	*Common bent*	*July-Aug.*
Aira Praecox	*Early hair grass*	*April-June*
Anagallis arvensis	*Scarlet pimpernel*	*June-Aug*
Armeria maritima*	*Sea pink*	*March-Sept.*
Asplenium marinum	*Sea spleenwort*	
Atriplex glabriuscula	*Babington's orache*	*July-Sept.*
Atriplex hastata*	*Hastate orache*	*Aug.-Sept.*
Beta vulgaris*	*Sea beet*	*July-Sept.*
Cerastium fontanum	*Common mouse-ear*	*April-Sept.*
Cerastium tetrandrum	*Dark green chickweed*	*April-Oct.*
Cirsium vulgare	*Spear thistle*	*July-Sept.*
Cochlearia officinalis*	*Common scurvy grass*	*May-Aug.*
Dryoptens dilatata	*Buckler fern*	
Festuca rubra	*Red fescue*	*May-June*
Holcus lanatus	*Yorkshire fog*	*May-Aug.*
Jasione montana	*Common sheep's bit*	*May-Aug.*
Juncus bufonius	*Toad rush*	
Leontodon autumnalis	*Smooth hawkbit*	*July-Oct.*
Plantago coronopus*	*Buck's-horn plantain*	*May-Aug.*
Plantago maritima	*Sea plantain*	*June-Aug.*
Poa annua	*Annual meadow grass*	*All year*
Poa trivialis	*Rough meadow grass*	*June-July*
Polypodium vulgare	*Common polypody*	
Rumex acetosa	*Common sorrel*	*May-June*
Rumex crispus	*Curled dock*	*June-Oct.*
Sagina maritima	*Sea pearlwort*	*May-Sept.*
Sagina procumbens	*Common pearlwort*	*May-Oct.*
Sedum anglicum	*English stonecrop*	*June-Aug.*
Senecio jacobaea	*Ragwort*	*July-Aug.*
Silene maritima*	*Sea campion*	*June-Aug.*
Sonchus asper	*Prickly sowthistle*	*June-Aug.*
Sonchus oleraceus	*Common sowthistle*	*June-Aug.*
Spergularia rupicola*	*Rock sea spurrey*	*June-Sept.*
Stellaria media	*Chickweed*	*All year*
Trifolium repens	*White clover*	*May-Oct.*
Tripleurospermum maritimum*	*Scentless chamomile*	*July-Sept.*
Umbilicus rupestris	*Wall pennywort*	*June-Aug.*

* Plants also found on Small Skellig.

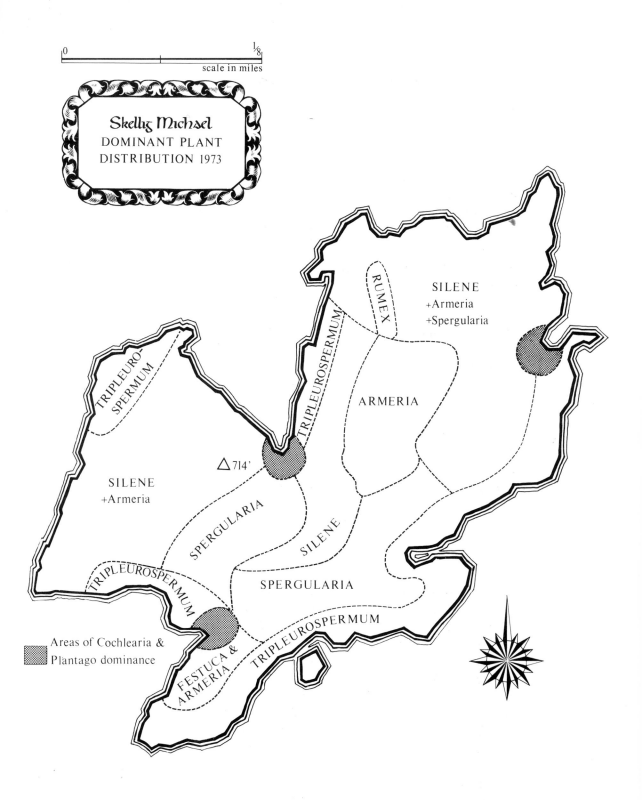

Underwater photographers at Skellig have a good
opportunity to study the Atlantic Grey Seals
at close quarters.

Skellig's Seals

Passing near Skellig by boat, one cannot miss the island's Grey seals (Halichoerus grypus). They spend their summer days basking on the rock ledges or fishing adroitly in the surrounding seas.

Twenty was the greatest number of Grey seals I have ever seen on the rocks at the one time — and that was in mid-September, 1971. One big, conspicuous bull seal — with that characteristic, humped nose — occupied the highest position in the herd, and many, straight-nosed expectant female Greys — only a few weeks away from pupping time — lay about nearer the water's edge.

How convenient that it is by their noses — the only part which is visible as they swim — that seals are identified. Had there been any of Ireland's other seal, the Common seal (Phoca vitulina) in the area, their pert, upturned noses would have been their identification.

Inquisitive creatures are seals, as has often been noted by aqualung divers in the area. Swimming up close to a diver, the seals will stare at him in what appears to be stark, wide-eyed disbelief, and then dash away again — only to repeat the performance in a moment. One wonders if they would be so entertaining and playful at the end of September when their new, white 30 lb. pups have arrived.

One wonders too at a time like this if there is any justice for Ireland's 2,000 Grey seals and their annual 460 pups — a price on their heads as alleged salmon killers? Anyone who has ever sailed near the Small Skellig on a fine day and drifted a while to study the sleek, grey, bewhiskered forms, or anyone who has found that he himself is under close scrutiny as another big-eyed, wide-nostrilled, black head pops up a few feet away from the boat, will feel that there must be ways of protecting salmon stocks other than the incessant shooting of these beautiful beasts on various other parts of our coast.

Well camouflaged by their natural colours, grey
seals bask in the sunshine on Small Skellig.

Underwater World

For those of us who have the opportunity to extend our exploration of Skellig to the underwater world, there is much reward. The seals, the giant, harmless Basking shark, the shoals of pollack and mackerel, the defiant lobsters, the proud crawfish and the rich colours of the anemone-clad rock faces create a silent moonscape of remarkable beauty. The whims of wind, weather and tide add to the infinite variety of this area, and it is little wonder that in the short space of years since aqualung diving has become a popular sport, the name of Skellig has become famous in the diving circles of Europe.

Skellig is a place for experienced divers only. Its underwater cliffs plunge downward in sheer, vertical faces to a depth of 70 metres where they finally become part of that gently-sloping, rock-strewn plateau which is the Continental Shelf, and many factors other than the capacity of one's air cylinders govern the time which may be spent admiring the underwater world.

Depth, (pressure), and time impose a very exact limit to the amount of diving one can do in a day, and to exceed this table is to court death or crippling disablement from 'the bends'. Cold is another factor. Skellig waters are well tempered by the Gulf Stream but even though the surface temperature may be 16°C. on a summer's day, the layers 30 metres down may be as low as 10°. Notwithstanding the efficient insulation of modern diving suits, such cold can ultimately bring many attendant hazards.

Visitors who come to Skellig for its Archaeology or Ornithology frequently view divers with some perplexity when these black-suited figures slip into the sea and disappear in a trail of bubbles. "What on earth are they looking for?" is the immediate question.

"Fanfare" Macro photo from the head of a
marine worm. (Length of tendrils:
approx. 60 mm.)

The answer is complex, and perhaps one needs to be a diver to appreciate it. Here, lapping our own shore, is a world as alien as the moon — yet full of life, full of history — possibly full of indications for the future — just waiting to be explored. We can learn from it; we can live from it; if we came from it, perhaps we can go back to it some day. There is a new maturity of thought in the diving world; the speargun has been rejected; the underwater cameras, with light meters, flash equipment and all the trappings of successful photography, have been embraced by many for an orderly, intelligent approach to a new frontier.

It was a quirk of Skellig weather which led three Limerick divers to an interesting find in the spring of 1975.

John, Martin and Noel are on board the diving boat *Béal Bocht*. The wind is North-East, force 4, which means that they must dive on the West side of the islands. Small Skellig, with its interesting seal coves, is the choice.

"Mardi Gras". Close-up studies of minute marine worms give a vivid impression of colourful fireworks. (The approximate length of the tendrils: 60 mm.).

Experienced divers, they kit up with the full array of equipment: suit, life jacket, aqualung, weight belt, knife, watch, depth gauge, compass, fins, mask, snorkel.... Lamp in hand, they slip over the side and are gone.

Down the steep rock-face they glide, swimming through a 3-metre high forest of gold and red weed. The yellow colours begin to disappear as they descend, then the reds. There is still ample light, and horizontal visibility is 12 metres or more, but gradually everything becomes blue. The divers switch on their lamps to compensate for this colour filtration, and immediately all the glorious red and yellow sponges and the green and turquoise anemones come back to vivid life.

It is silent here. The only audible sound is the two-tone hiss of respiration and exhaust bubbles. A seal swims into view, grey and ghostly, and suddenly is gone again — totally masterful in his own environment.

Portrait of a Skellig citizen — the crawfish.
(Size of this fish: approximately 1 kg.)

"The cold, baleful stare of a conger eel".
(Approximate size of this fish: 1.5m.)

At 25 metres, the seaweed begins to thin out and only a few barren stalks remain. A shoal of pollack passes overhead, reducing the weak daylight to almost nil. The divers pause and watch the intricate, army-like movements of the shoal: "Left turn. Right turn." To some unheard command, ten thousand fish turn as one, synchronised to a fraction of a second. "About turn. Slow march." The shoal moves on....

Now the divers are in the bottom of a gully, 30 metres below the surface; there is little or no weed growing at this depth and the surrounding water is deathly still — but it is a deceptive stillness; the smooth polish on the rock face is indicative of the savage abrasions of sand and boulders during winter storms.

A spotted dogfish — lazy offshoot of the shark family — lumbers into the scene and flops down on a flat rock for a rest. Bleary-eyed and lethargic in appearance, he is reluctant to be disturbed, and even when the divers swim up close to study him he moves on only a few metres, and rests again.

From the dim cavern beneath a large boulder, the cold, baleful stare of a conger eel is fixed on the three approaching newcomers. Steel-blue body, white mane erect along the length of his back, the conger is powerful, fearsome and sinister — but he tends to mind his own business if he is left unmolested.

A huge angler-fish, perfectly camouflaged in his grey mottling, lies on the shingle between the rocks, his mouth — almost as wide as his body is long — wide agape. His 'fishing rod' dangles from his nose as a bait to entice smaller fry within range of his razor-sharp teeth. He is another one best left alone!

The divers continue along the crevasse, checking time and depth frequently. Here is a lobster in resplendant blue, aggressive and un-afraid; he raises his claws and challenges the intruders. There in the shelter of an overhanging ledge is a fragile rose-coral in muted apricot. Here is a crawfish in sunset red, clinging to a pointed crag. He shoots off backwards out of sight with a few powerful thrusts of his tail. Left or right, up or down, an indescribable variety of colour blazes on every side when touched by the pencil beam of the lights.

The three companions stop, rock-still, hardly breathing. Here is an ancient anchor and some fragments of rusted chain — and a cannon — and some lead pipes — and another cannon — and another.... A wreck at the Skellig! What ship was this? When was it lost? What hardship and misery did these sailors suffer in their final hours, with only the wild Atlantic for a grave, the gaunt rocks for a headstone, and the ever-screaming gannets for a dirge?

In the boat, we have been following the progress of the divers' bubbles, and finally the three men surface right beside our boarding ladder. "Cannons and anchors and lead plumbing...." They are agog with the news even before they climb out of the water. "The cannons are about eight feet in length... the lead pipe is about four inches in diameter.... the anchors are long and have strange-shaped flukes...." It seemed like a big joke or a dream, and we were not quite prepared to believe that after some ten years of diving and exploration in this area, the Skellig had finally yielded an unknown wreck!

The temptation was great. Everyone wanted a cannon for his front lawn.... and the lead pipe would have a good value as scrap... But a different policy was adopted. A small sample of the lead was lifted for chemical analysis and to photograph a rather ornate plumber's joint. One cannon ball was removed for preservation, and for the duration of the summer's diving in the area, the motto was "search and report".

It will take more summers at Skellig before anyone can determine the extent or the significance of this site, but preliminary pointers suggest a small vessel of the 18th/19th century, and it is possible that we are looking at the resting place of that 97 ton, single-decked brig, constructed by Capt. and Co. at Lowestoft in 1802, owned and skippered by Mr. J. Sterry, last surveyed in 1834, registered in London and named *The Lady Nelson*.

I'm not sure that I really want to know for certain. For me it is exciting to have one more Skellig question which does not have a concrete answer.

"Anemone-clad rock faces create a silent moonscape of remarkable beauty".
(Approx. diameter of this anemone: 35mm)

Extensive masonry-fall in front of Cell A. This damage has gone unattended for years.

A Hundred Years From Now

uch are the Skellig rocks — Skellig Michael and Small Skellig — 8½ miles off Valentia on the Atlantic coast of Kerry, not our properties, but nonetheless our individual and collective responsibilities. What does the future hold for these islands, say ten, fifty, a hundred years from now? Can the ancient buildings which braved the Vikings, and some fifteen hundred years of Atlantic storms, survive an ever-increasing tourist traffic, and go unscathed in this unsupervised outpost, or will the same uneasy Atlantic be a limiting factor — a safety valve — to the number of visitors Skellig can receive in any one season?

If the Skellig lighthouse ever becomes automatic, who will keep that occasional "fatherly eye" on the condition of the monastery buildings, so that timely preventative measures — rather than impossible restorative works — may be undertaken?

The more immediate question is: Can the monastery buildings survive the depredation of the island's rabbits? Already their burrowing has precipitated such rock-falls that the lighthouse road near Cross Cove had to be roofed for safety, and the old road to the upper lighthouse had to be closed as "dangerous". Some recent damage to the monastery is clearly apparent, and one shudders to think of the example of Church Island in Valentia harbour where rabbits have undermined and destroyed similar ancient buildings in a very short period of time. The Board of Public Works, guardian of the Skellig archaeology, has been aware of the damage on Skellig for at least three years, if further time and neglect cause an extension of the Skellig masonry-falls, the criminal carelessness of that Board will not easily be forgiven.

The birds — will they always be unmolested, unpolluted? The leasing of Small Skellig as an official wild bird refuge is a welcome action, but is that enough? The world's largest oil-tankers are sailing into Bantry bay, 20 miles away, yet it seems that this country has pathetic contingency plans in the event of a tanker mishap or a major oil spillage.

History and Nature have placed their priceless and irreplaceable treasures in our hands, and have given us a heavy responsibility. Will generations yet-unborn indict or vindicate our stewardship?

"Tread carefully on Skellig" is a good motto.

An Irish Lights tender at Skellig with fuel and heavy stores.

Bibliography

The Skelligs and many aspects of these two islands are reported in various languages and many publications too numerous to mention. These are my principal and most useful references:

Ancient History of the Kingdom of Kerry, by Friar O'Sullivan of Muckross Abbey, ed. by Fr. J. Prendergast (J. Cork H.A.S. 1900), pp. 152 ff.

Annals of Innisfallen, ed. Sean Mac Airt (1951) pp. 124-25, 136-37, 208-09.

Annals of the Kingdom of Ireland by the Four Masters, ed. O'Donovan, pp. 666-67.

Annals of Ulster, ed. W. Hennessey, vol. I, pp. 318-10.

Antiquarian Handbook, R.S.A.I., 1904, ed. R. Cochrane.

Charlesworth, *The Geology of Ireland,* Oliver & Boyd, 1953.

Chatterton, *Rambles in the South of Ireland,* vol. I, 1839. Publ: Saunders & Otley.

De Paor, *A Survey of Sceilig Mhichil, J.R.S.A.I.,* 1955.

De Paor, *Early Christian Ireland,* Thames & Hudson, 1960.

Dunraven, *Notes on Ir. Arch.,* vol. I (ed. by M. Stokes), George Bell & Sons, 1875.

Fisher, *The Fulmar,* London Collins, 1952.

Fisher and Vevers, *The Journal of Animal Ecology, Nos. 11, 12, 1943.*

Foley, *The Ancient and Present State of the Skelligs, Blasket Islands, etc.,* 1903.

Giraldus Cambrensis, *In Topographia Hibernie,* ed. J. O'Meara.

Hayward, *In the Kingdom of Kerry,* 1946.

Henry, *Early Monasteries, Beehive Huts and Dry-stone Houses,* Proc. R.I.A.,

Jackson, *Scéalta ón mBlascaod,* An Cumann le Béaloideis na hEirinn.

J.R.S.A.I. 1892, J. Romilly Allen, pp. 277 ff.

Keating, *History of Ireland,* vol. I, lines 1342-46; vol. III, 1. 2480.

Keeble Martin, *The Concise British Flora in Colour,* Michael Joseph.

Kennedy, *The Birds of Ireland,* Oliver & Boyd

La Croix, *John Paul Jones,* Muller, 1962.

Lewis, *Topographical Directory of Ireland, 1837*

Lockley; *The Irish Naturalist's Journal, Vol. 15, No. V, 1966.*

Martyrology of Tallaght, (Henry Bradshaw Society, vol. LXVIII),

Matthews, *British Mammals,* Collins, London.

Maxwell, *A Book of Islands,* Bell & Sons, London, 1945.

McClintock, *Old Irish and Highland Dress.* Dundalgan.

Morris, *A History of British Birds,* (8 vols.), Groombridge.

Newman J.H. *Historical Sketches,* III — Longmans, 1917.

O'Crohan, *The Islandman,* Talbot, 1937.

O'Donoghue, *Brendaninia, 1870.*

O'Gorman, *Breeding Stations of the Grey Seal,* Bulletin Mamm. Soc., 1963.

O'Rourke, *The Fauna of Ireland,* Mercier.

Peterson, *A Field Guide to the Birds of Britain and Ireland,* Collins, 1966.

Praeger, *The Botanist in Ireland,* Hodges & Figgis, 1934.

Praeger, *The Natural History of Ireland,* Dundalk, 1950.

Praeger, *The Way That I Went,* Allen Figgis, 1969.

Reade, *Nesting Birds,* Blandford.

Scully, *Flora of County Kerry,* Hodges & Figgis, 1916.

Seamus Dubh, ed., *The Songs of Tomas Ruadh O'Sullivan,* Gill, 1914.

Smith, *The Ancient and Present State of the County of Kerry, 1756.*

Westropp, Proc. R.S.A.I. 1897, p. 308-135.

Wilson, *The Irish Lighthouse Service,* Allen & Figgis, 1968.

Wynne, *Geological Survey of Ireland, H.M.S.O., 1861.*

This beautiful cross just
off the principal Southern
climb blends so well with
its background that it is
seldom noticed.
(The background has been
omitted here to show the
cross more clearly).

Index

Illustrations

END PAPERS are from an engraving of Skellig Michael taken from *Irish Pictures* by Richard Lovett, London 1888.

CAPITAL LETTERS at the beginning of each chapter are taken from *Manuscripts of Ireland* by John T. Gilbert. The letters were originally reproduced from the following manuscripts, *Leabhar Mor Duna Doighre c.* 1390 and *The Book of Ballimote Fourteenth Century,* both in the Royal Irish Academy.

Slabs and crosses in "the monk's graveyard".